Super Soups

First hard-copy edition published 2011

Disclaimer
This manual is not intended to provide medical advice or to take the place of medical advice and treatment from your personal physician. Readers are advised to consult their own doctors or other qualified health professionals regarding the treatment of medical conditions. The author shall not be held liable or responsible for any misunderstanding or misuse of the information contained in this manual or for any loss, damage, or injury caused or alleged to be caused directly or indirectly by any treatment, action, or application of any food or food source discussed in this manual. The statements in this book have not been evaluated by the U.S. Food and Drug Administration. This information is not intended to diagnose, treat, cure, or prevent any disease.
To request permission for reproduction or inquire about private nutritional consulting or speaking engagements, contact:

Isabel De Los Rios
Live Smart Solutions Inc.
2345 7th Street
Denver, CO 80211
E-mail: questions@beyonddiet.com

Contents

Introduction

This guide includes some delicious soup recipes, submitted by our very own Beyond Diet customers. All recipes have been thoroughly reviewed and approved by me to ensure that each one follows all Beyond Diet requirements.

Because Beyond Diet does promote the inclusion of many different foods into your daily meal plans, it is essential to keep your soups new, fun and interesting. Eating the same foods again and again leads to boredom and abandonment. To prevent this from happening, I highly encourage you to try at least one new recipe per week that suits your meal plan. Also, be adventurous and try some foods that you have never tried before.

Also, remember that allowable food servings and portion sizes differ for each person, depending on metabolism type and the number of calories required daily. Please adjust recipe portions to suit your meal plan, as instructed in the Chapter on Daily Meal Planning, according to the Allowable Servings Guide and the Food Choices charts. For example, if you are a Carb Type allowed four 1-oz servings of protein for dinner and a soup recipe calls for 6 oz of chicken (or doesn't specify a portion size), eat only 4 oz of chicken with your meal. You do not need to be this precise all the time, especially if several different ingredients are included in your soup. It is best to listen to your body and pay attention to hunger/fullness cues.

Remember, fresh food is best, and the more whole and natural the food you eat, the healthier you will be—and the better you will feel. Enjoy your delicious soups!

With all of the recipes presented here (and with any other recipe you may choose to use), adhere to all the principles taught in the manual. Here are a few points to remember and consider for each recipe:

Go Organic	Organic ingredients are always best.
Salt	Use an unrefined sea salt or, preferably, Celtic sea salt or Redmond's Real Salt. http://go.beyonddiet.com/SGetCelticSeaSalt
Oils	The best oils to use for cooking are coconut oil, butter or ghee. http://go.beyonddiet.com/SGetCoconutOil
Water	Water should be pure and filtered. http://go.beyonddiet.com/SGetWaterFiltration
Honey	Honey should always be raw. http://go.beyonddiet.com/SGetRawHoney
Sweeteners	Stevia or Xylitol can be used instead of raw honey. http://go.beyonddiet.com/SGetStevia
Nuts & Seeds	Nuts and seeds should always be raw and preferably organic. Cooking and/or roasting nuts damages the health benefits of raw nuts. If you are going to roast your own nuts, use the lowest temperature possible (preferably below 300 degrees) and even that will do some damage to the nuts, so choose raw whenever possible. http://go.beyonddiet.com/SGetNutsandSeeds
General Ingredients	Fresh ingredients with minimal processing are always best.
Yogurt	Yogurt should be full fat and organic.
Butter	Organic butter from grass fed cows is your best choice. http://go.beyonddiet.com/SGetRawButter

Chicken Soups

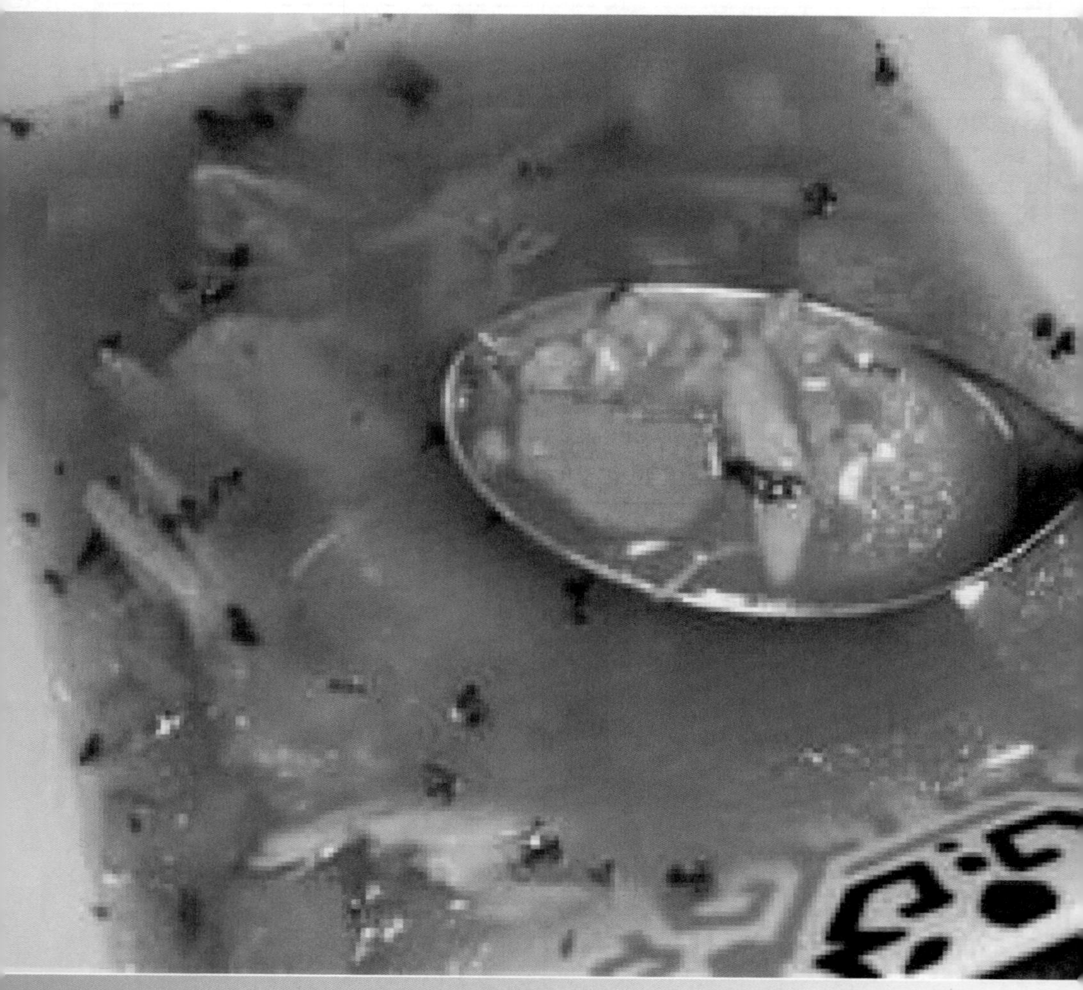

Award-Winning Chicken Soup

Servings: 16
Proteins/Carbs/Fats: 2 / 1 / 0

Ingredients

3 Tbsp Olive Oil

6 stalks Celery (sliced)

6 Large Carrots (sliced)

1 Large Onion (sliced)

1 Whole Chicken (cut up) or 1 Large Package of Chicken Parts (any you want)

1 Large Bunch Parsley (minced)

2-3 Large Garlic Cloves (peeled and smashed)

5-6 (14.5 oz) cans Chicken Broth (enough to cover all ingredients in the pot)

To taste Unrefined Sea Salt and Pepper

Directions

Place olive oil in a large soup pot and turn heat on medium. Saute all the celery, carrots, and onion until translucent.

Add all of the chicken on top of the veggies. Put all of the parsley in the pot. Add the peeled, smashed garlic cloves to the top of the pile. Pour in enough chicken stock to cover all of the ingredients. Add salt and pepper, to taste.

Give it all a great big stir.

Cook over low heat for 35 minutes until the chicken is no longer pink. Stir occasionally.

Submitted by: Vicki Kron

Kerin's Chicken & Coconut Soup

Servings: 4
Proteins/Carbs/Fats: 1 / 0 / 0

Ingredients

1/2 cup Brown Rice

3 cups Chicken Broth

1 (14 oz) can Coconut Milk

2 Tbsp Curry Powder

1 Red Chili Pepper (minced)

1 Medium Parsnip (diced)

3 Small Chicken Breast (cut in 1/2 inch strips)

4 Tbsp Lime Juice

1 Spring Onion

To taste Coriander (chopped)

To taste Unrefined Sea Salt & Black Pepper

Directions

Cook the rice.

Bring the chicken broth, coconut milk, curry, and chili to a boil.

Add the parsnip and simmer for 5 minutes.

Add the chicken and cook until done, about 6-8 minutes.

Add the rice and simmer for 30 seconds.

Remove from heat.

Add the lime juice, salt, and pepper to taste.

Garnish with chopped spring onion, coriander, and lime slices.

Enjoy!

Submitted by: Kerin Black - Stuttgart, Germany

Vicki's Chicken Soup

Servings: 6
Proteins/Carbs/Fats: 5 / 1 / 0

Ingredients

1 (3 lb) Whole Organic Chicken (cut into pieces)

2 quarts Water

1 Large Onion (chopped)

2 stalks Organic Celery with Leaves (chopped)

1/2 cup Chopped Fresh Parsley

5 Black Peppercorns

1 Bay Leaf

1/4 tsp Celery Seed

1 pinch Dried Thyme

1 tsp Unrefined Sea Salt

Directions

In a large pot combine chicken, water, large onion, celery with leaves, fresh parsley, peppercorns, bay leaf, celery seeds, thyme and 1 teaspoon salt. Bring to a boil, then reduce heat, cover and simmer 4 hours.

Strain stock, reserving chicken, and refrigerate for 1 hour or until fat can be skimmed off top.

Skim fat from top of stock. Remove skin and bones from chicken and cut meat into bite-size pieces. Return stock and chicken to pot and stir in carrots, 1/2 cup sliced celery, 1/4 cup minced onion, fresh parsley, 1 teaspoon salt, pepper and rice. Bring to a boil, then reduce heat and simmer 30 minutes.

Submitted by: Vicki - Topeka, Kansas

Rick's Quick Chicken Rice Soup

Servings: 12-14
Proteins/Carbs/Fats: 2 / 1 / 0

Ingredients

3 1/2 quarts Water

3-4 stalks Celery (chopped)

16 oz Carrots (peeled and chopped)

1/2 Onion (chopped)

2 Boneless Chicken Breasts (chopped)

3 Tbsp Better Than Bouillon Organic Chicken Base

1 Tbsp Italian Seasoning

1 Tbsp Garlic Powder

1 tsp Black Pepper (optional)

1/2 cup Wild or Brown Rice (uncooked)

Directions

Start by boiling 1 quart of water and add the celery to soften them up while you cut up the carrots, onion and chicken.

Next add the carrots and onion and bring back to a boil. Add the remaining ingredients and simmer for about 30 minutes.

When the rice is soft, you are ready to eat!

Submitted by: Rick Stensberg - Wisconsin Rapids, WI

White Chicken Chili

Servings: 6
Proteins/Carbs/Fats: 3 / 1 / 1

Ingredients

4 cups Chicken Breast (chopped and cooked)

2 Tbsp Olive Oil

1 Medium Onion

3 cloves Garlic

1 Red Pepper

2 Tbsp Fresh Parsley

1-2 Tbsp Chili Powder

2 tsp Cumin

1 tsp Unrefined Sea Salt

1 (32 oz) carton Organic Chicken Broth

2 cans Organic Great Northern Beans

2 Tbsp Fresh Cilantro

2 Tbsp Arrowroot

1 cup Organic Heavy Cream (preferably raw)

Directions

Chop onion in food processor. Heat olive oil and saute onion until soft. Add garlic, red pepper and parsley to food processor then add to pan. Add chili powder, cumin and salt. Saute until vegetables are soft and spices are blended. Add chicken broth and cut up chicken breasts to pan. Rinse and drain canned beans. Add to pan. Bring to a boil and simmer for about 30 to 40 minutes. Chop fresh cilantro and add to pan. Cook 10-15 minutes longer. Place arrowroot powder in small bowl. Gradually stir in heavy cream until well combined. Then gradually stir this mixture into hot soup, stirring constantly until soup is thickened and combined. Serve in bowls garnished with fresh cilantro or parsley.

Submitted by: Sharon Graham - Chespeake, Virginia

Mullagatawny Soup

Servings: 12
Proteins/Carbs/Fats: 2 / 1 / 0

Ingredients

4 tbsp Butter

1 1/2 lb Chicken Thighs (diced, boneless, skinless)

2 Tbsp Garam Masala (mild)

1 3/4 tsp Sea Salt

2 cups Onions (diced small)

1/2 cup Carrots (diced small)

1/2 cup Celery (diced small)

2 Tbsp Garlic (minced)

2 Tbsp Ginger (minced)

2 cups Granny Smith Apples (peeled, cored and diced)

1 cup Yukon Gold Potaotes (peeled and diced)

1 cup Sweet Potatoes (peeled and diced)

6 cups Chicken or Beef Stock

3/4 tsp Freshly Ground Black Pepper

1 cup Tightly Packed Baby Spinach

1 (14oz) can Unsweetened Coconut Milk

1 cup Chopped Tomatoes (canned with juice)

1/2 cup Cilantro (chopped)

Directions

Set a 4 or 5-quart saucepan over medium heat and add the butter. While the butter is heating, season the chicken with the garam masala and 1/4 teaspoon of the salt. Once the butter is hot, add the chicken and cook, turning often, until golden brown and fragrant, 6-8 minutes. Transfer the chicken to a plate and set aside to cool.

While the chicken is cooling, add the onions, carrots and celery to the hot pan and saute until lightly caramelized, about 4-5 minutes.

Add the garlic, ginger and apples to the pan and saute until the apples are caramelized, about 7-8 minutes. Add the potatoes and sweet potatoes to the pan, along with 4 cups of the chicken stock.

Raise the heat to high and bring to a boil.

Reduce to a simmer and cook the soup until the potatoes are tender, about 10 minutes. Add the reserved chicken, the remaining 1 1/2 teaspoons salt, the pepper, remaining 2 cups of chicken stock, spinach, cilantro and tomatoes.

Continue to cook the soup at a simmer until the chicken is tender, 10 minutes longer. Remove from the heat and stir in the coconut milk. Taste and adjust seasoning, if necessary.

Submitted by: Laura Cotnoir

Momma Mia's Chicken Soup

Servings: 4
Proteins/Carbs/Fats: 2 / 2 / 0

Ingredients

3 cloves Garlic (chopped)

1 Onion (chopped)

4 Tbsp Olive Oil or Coconut Oil

4 stalks Celery Hearts (sliced)

1 cup Baby Carrots (sliced)

1 large can Peeled Tomatoes (diced with juice)

2 Skinless Chicken Breasts

To taste Unrefined Sea Salt & Fresh Ground Black Pepper

To taste Dried Parsley, Basil and Oregano

Directions

In a large pan sauté oil, garlic, and onion. Add tomatoes and simmer.

Add about 2/3 cups filtered water.

Add celery and carrots. Simmer at medium heat for 15 minutes.

Add chicken breasts whole. Add seasonings and cook at medium heat for 1 hour or until a little reduced.

Remove chicken & shred the meat using 2 forks.

Return the shredded meat to soup and simmer for 15 minutes. Season using salt, pepper, dried parsley, basil and oregano.

Submitted by: Joe - Spring Hill, Florida

Italian Chicken Soup

Servings: 7
Proteins/Carbs/Fats: 4 / 1 / 0

Ingredients

3 Tbsp Olive Oil, Butter or Ghee

1 Onion (diced)

3 cloves Garlic (chopped)

3 Medium Carrots (peeled and diced)

2 Celery Ribs (diced)

1 tsp Unrefined Sea Salt

3/4 tsp Freshly Ground Black Pepper

3 1/2 cups Chicken Broth

1/2 cup Packed Basil Leaves (chopped) or 1 Tbsp Dried

2 Tbsp Tomato Paste

1 Bay Leaf

2 Large Chicken Breasts with Skin and Bones (about 1.75 lbs)

2 1/2 cups Frozen Italian Green Beans (thawed)

1 (15 oz) can Cannellini Beans (rinsed and drained)

Directions

In a large, heavy saucepan, heat the oil over medium-high heat. Add the carrots, celery, onion, garlic, salt and pepper, and cook until the onion is translucent (about 5 minutes). Stir in the chicken broth, basil, tomato paste and bay leaf.

Add the chicken and press down to submerge. Bring the liquid to a simmer. Reduce the heat to medium low, and simmer. Cover. Turn the chicken over and stir occasionally for 20 minutes. Add the thawed Italian green beans and the cannellini beans and simmer until the chicken is cooked, about 10 minutes. Turn off the heat. Remove the chicken and let cool for 10 minutes.

Discard the skin and bones and cut the meat into bite-size pieces. Return the meat to the saucepan and simmer for 5 minutes until warmed through. Remove bay leaf. Season with additional salt and pepper if desired.

Submitted by: Marianne - Branford, Florida

Chicken & Sausage Soup

Servings: 8
Proteins/Carbs/Fats: 4 / 1 / 0

Ingredients

1 lb Chicken Thighs or Breast (cut in long medium sized strips)

1 lb Italian Sausage (spicy or mild)

1/2 bag Baby Carrots

3 Celery Stalks

1/2 Onion

1/2 cup Cauliflower Florets

1 can Kidney Beans (rinsed)

1 Tbsp Garlic

2 cups Chicken Broth

1 Chicken Oxo (if more flavor is desired)

To taste Pepper & Garlic Spice

Directions

Cut chicken into long medium-sized strips. Turn crockpot to high heat. Put chicken into crockpot, cover, and let cook.

While chicken cooks, broil sausage in oven, allowing fat to drip off. When it is cooked (about 15 minutes) cut up the sausage. Then put on top of chicken in crock pot.

Add carrots, chopped celery, florets of cauliflower, onion, garlic and spices.

Mix chicken oxo with 1 cup chicken broth; pour over everything in crockpot. Then pour last cup of chicken broth. into crockpot. Finally, add the kidney beans.

Cook at high heat for about 4-5 hours.

*Add whatever spices (or none at all) to suit your tastebuds! Enjoy!

Submitted by: Marianne - Branford, Florida

Chicken & Vegetable Soup

Servings: 4
Proteins/Carbs/Fats: 4 / 2 / 0

Ingredients

12 cups Organic Chicken Broth

7 cups Filtered Water

1 cup Brown Rice

1 cup Onions (chopped)

4 Medium Carrots (cut into 1/4 inch rounds)

2 Medium Zucchini (cut into 1/2 inch pieces)

2 Medium Yellow Squash (cut into 1/2 inch pieces)

1 lb Cooked Chicken (chopped)

12 oz Frozen Organic Peas

2 tsp Unrefined Sea Salt

1 tsp Pepper

Directions

In an 8 quart pot, bring the chicken broth to a boil. Lower the setting to medium. Add the rice. Cook for 20 minutes.

Add the onion and carrots and cook for 10 minutes.

Add the zucchini and yellow squash. Cook for 15 minutes.

Add the cooked chicken and peas. Boil another 5 minutes or until heated through.

Add the salt and pepper to taste.

Submitted by: Terri Galindo

Thai Soup

Servings: 2
Proteins/Carbs/Fats: 4 / 1 / 0

Ingredients

1 tsp Ginger

2 tsp Fish Sauce

1 can Chicken Stock

1 can Coconut Milk

1 Serrano Pepper

1/4 Large Sweet Onion (or 1/2 small sweet onion)

2 Scallions

1 tsp Stevia (or to taste)

1/2 lb Chicken Tenders or Chicken Breast

1/2 large package Mushrooms (or 1 whole small package)

1 Lime (juiced)

1/2 bunch Cilantro

Directions

Peel the ginger and slice it into thin rounds. Put it in the wok. Add the can of chicken stock and the fish sauce. Turn on the heat to medium or high until it bubbles. Then turn the heat down to low and cover for 15 minutes. Add the coconut milk at the finish of the 15 minutes. Stir and then let it cook another 5 minutes. Then slice the serrano pepper into thick rounds, and put them in the wok. Let simmer while you chop up the sweet onion and scallions. Once they are chopped, add them to the wok. Stir them in along with the stevia. Let that simmer further while you cut up the chicken into bite size pieces. Add the chicken once it's chopped. Stir it around.

When you see the pieces of chicken getting white, cover the wok and let it cook another 5-10 minutes until the chicken is cooked through. While that is cooking cut off the stalks of the mushrooms, and then slice them into small rounds. Also, cut the lime in half. Add the mushrooms once you think the chicken is cooked or mostly cooked. Squeeze the lime halves into the wok. Let this simmer while you chop the cilantro roughly. Add it to the wok.

At this point, you can serve whenever you feel the soup has simmered long enough to taste. Enjoy!

*This recipe is spicy with the serranos. So, if you don't love spiciness, you may want to at least cut out the seeds. If you love spiciness, leave the serranos whole, but cut into large rounds, and add even more of your favorite hot sauce later if you like.

Submitted by: Helen Powell-Bagge

Spicy Chicken Spinach Soup

Servings: 4
Proteins/Carbs/Fats: 3 / 1 / 0

Ingredients

1 Tbsp Olive Oil

1/2 cup Celery (chopped)

1 Small Bunch Scallions (chopped, some green as well as white)

1/2 tsp Unrefined Sea Salt

1/4 tsp Ground Pepper

4 cans (15 oz) Reduced Sodium Chicken Broth

2 Boneless, Skinless Chicken Breasts (cooked and cut in 1/2 inch cubes)

1 (10 oz) bag Fresh Baby Spinach

1 small can Chopped Green Chiles

1 Tbsp Lemon Juice

1/2 cup Sliced Almonds (for garnish)

Directions

In a large pot, heat oil over medium heat.

Add celery and cook 5 minutes, until it is wilted.

Add scallions, salt, and pepper, and cook 5 minutes more.

Add chicken broth and bring to a boil over medium-high heat; simmer 5 minutes.

Add chopped chicken breasts, chopped green chiles, and spinach and simmer 5 minutes until chicken and chiles are warmed through and spinach is wilted.

Add lemon juice.

Place ¾ cup in each bowl and top with sliced almonds.

Submitted by: Pam Lindsay

Squash Soups

Spicy Pumpkin Soup

Servings: 4
Proteins/Carbs/Fats: 0 / 1 / 0

Ingredients

1 lb Pumpkin

3 cups Vegetable Stock or Broth

1 clove Garlic (minced)

Same amount Fresh Ginger (minced)

1-2 tsp Curry

1/2 cup Coconut Milk

To taste Unrefined Sea Salt

To taste Cayenne Pepper

For garnish Pumpkin Seeds

Directions

Cut the pumpkin into approximately 1-inch dices.

Cook with garlic and ginger in vegetable bouillon until tender (about 20 minutes).

Add curry and coconut milk. Purée everything in a food processor.

Add salt and cayenne pepper to taste.

Pour into bowls and garnish with some pumpkin seeds.

Submitted by: Liza - Bremen, Germany & Northport, Alabama

Diane's Orange Soup

Servings: 4
Proteins/Carbs/Fats: 1 / 1 / 0

Ingredients

1 small package Mini Carrots

1 Large Yam or Sweet Potato

1 piece Pumpkin or Calabash

Equal portions Carrots, Yams, and Pumpkin/Calabash

4 or 5 cloves Garlic

2 cups Almond Milk (or other type if preferred)

2 tsp Cinnamon

1 tsp Cumin

2 cups Chicken Broth

To taste Unrefined Sea SAlt and Pepper

Directions

Place first 4 ingredients in standard size crock pot. Add water to cover. Cook until tender.

Place in blender and blend until smooth.

Return to crockpot. Add remaining ingredients and simmer on low for 30 minutes. Add water if too thick.

*This recipe freezes very well. Store in 1 1/2 cup portions, stick it in the freezer, and whenever you need a nice tasty soup, you can heat it up quickly!

Submitted by: Diane Fletcher

Healthy Butternut Squash Soup

Servings: 4
Proteins/Carbs/Fats: 0 / 1 / 0

Ingredients

1 Medium Butternut Squash

For cooking Butter

1 Medium Onion (diced)

1 Small Potato (quartered)

2 cloves Garlic

To taste Unrefined Sea Salt and Freshly Ground Black Pepper

1 tsp Thyme (freshly chopped)

3 1/2 cups Vegetable Stock (homemade is best or low-sodium stock cubes)

1 handful Chives (chopped)

Directions

Peel the butternut squash, scoop out the seeds, and cut the flesh into think wedges.

Heat the butter in a large pan, then add the onion and cook on a low heat for about 2 minutes.

Add the butternut and potato and coat in the butter. Cook for 2 minutes on a medium heat. Add the garlic, salt and pepper to taste. Add stock and simmer 25 - 30 minutes.

Using a hand blender or food processor, blend thoroughly. Serve with the chopped chives sprinkled on top.

Submitted by: Virginia Hayes - Mid Glamorgan, UK

Butternut Squash, Pears & Coconut Milk Soup

Servings: 8
Proteins/Carbs/Fats: 0 / 1 / 0

Ingredients

1 Tbsp Olive Oil, Butter or Ghee

1 Large Onion (chopped)

8 cups Butternut Squash (peeled, sliced and cut in cubes)

2 cups Pears (peeled and cut in cubes)

10 drops Hot Sauce

1/2 tsp Cumin Powder

2 Tbsp Fresh Cilantro (coriander) or Fresh Parsley (can use dried)

2 (15 oz) boxes Chicken Broth

1 (9.5 oz) can Coconut Milk

1/2 Lime (crushed for its juice) or 1 Tbsp Lime Juice (from a bottle)

To taste Unrefined Sea Salt and Pepper

Directions

Heat oil in a large pot; cook the onion until translucent.

Add spices, squash, pears, chicken broth, cilantro and hot sauce to the pot.

Simmer gently for 20-25 minutes.

Add the lime juice and season with salt and pepper.

You can add more hot sauce to your taste (in your bowl).

Submitted by: Alain & Brigitte - Gatineau, Québec, Canada

Roasted Pumpkin Soup

Servings: 5
Proteins/Carbs/Fats: 0 / 1 / 0

Ingredients

2 cups Pumpkin (chopped)

4 Shallots

2 Carrots (chopped)

1 Medium Apple (peeled & sliced)

1 Medium Onion (chopped)

2 Large Cloves Garlic

2 Tbsp Olive Oil (optional)

1/2 tsp Cumin

1/2 tsp Ground Coriander

1/2-3/4 tsp Turmeric

2 1/2 cups Low Sodium Vegetable Broth

Directions

Preheat oven to 425° F.

On large cookie sheet spread out all veggies in single layer. Combine spices with olive oil and drizzle over apple slices and veggies (or just mix the spices and sprinkle over the veggies).

Toss to coat.

Roast in oven for 20-25 minutes until veggies are tender.

Transfer all to blender, then add broth and blend until smooth.

Makes 5 one cup servings.

Submitted by: Cindy Barnett

Potato Pumpkin Soup

Servings: 7
Proteins/Carbs/Fats: 0 / 1 / 0

Ingredients

1 Large Piece of Pumpkin (peeled and chopped into chunks)

3 Potatoes (peeled and chopped into chunks)

2 Diced Brown Onions

3-4 cloves Garlic (minced)

1-2 tsp Curry Powder

4-5 cups Chicken Stock

2-3 Tbsp Tomato Paste

2 Tbsp Olive Oil, Butter or Ghee

To serve Cream or Yogurt

Chives (optional)

Directions

Saute onions till translucent on low heat.

Add garlic and stir for a minute.

Add pumpkin and potatoes (could also add cauliflower), and stir to combine.

Add chicken stock and curry powder; simmer till all vegetables are soft.

Turn heat off and add tomato paste.

Puree with hand blender.

Serve with a cream or yoghurt.

Garnish with some chopped chives.

Enjoy!

Submitted by: Del - Sydney, Australia

Jacqueline's Winter Vegetable Soup

Servings: 10
Proteins/Carbs/Fats: 0 / 1 / 0

Ingredients

1 Large Spanish (sweet) Onion (diced)

2 Leeks (white part only, sliced)

1 Apple + 1 Pear (chopped, Macintosh & Bartlett)

3 Yellow Zucchini (sliced)

1 Butternut Squash (chopped)

1 Sweet Potato (or yam, chopped)

2 Carrots

5-6 cups Vegetable Broth

1 Tbsp Olive Oil + 1 Tbsp Butter

1/2 tsp Allspice

1 tsp Caraway Seeds

Directions

Sauté the onion and leek in oil and butter mix.

Add chopped apple and pear, sauté until soft.

Add all the vegetables, the broth and seasonings.

Simmer for 45 minutes.

When the mixture has cooled, purée in a blender.

Submitted by: Jacqueline - Quebec, Canada

Apple Squash Soup

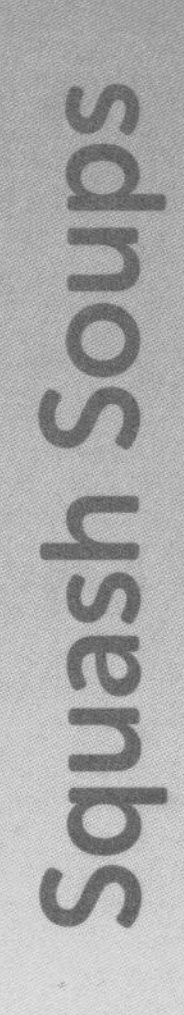

Servings: 8
Proteins/Carbs/Fats: 0 / 1 / 0

Ingredients

1 Tbsp Coconut Oil, Butter or Ghee

1 Onion (chopped)

1 clove Garlic (chopped)

3 lbs Butternut Squash (peeled and diced, about 3 cups)

1 Sweet Potato (peeled and diced, about 1 lb)

2 Apples (peeled, cored and diced)

4 cups Chicken or Vegetable Stock

1 Tbsp Fresh Thyme (chopped) or 1 tsp dried

1 Tbsp Fresh Rosemary (chopped) or 1 tsp dried

1 tsp Unrefined Sea Salt

1/4 tsp Pepper

3/4 cup Raw Milk or Coconut Milk (optional)

Directions

Heat oil over medium heat in a stock pot or large pot. Add onions, garlic and cook gently 2-3 minutes or until soft and fragrant.

Add squash, sweet potato and apples. Stir to combine. Add next 5 ingredients. Bring to boil. Reduce heat, cover and simmer for 30 minutes or until squash is very tender.

Puree soup. Return to low heat for 5 minutes to warm soup. Stir in milk if using. Taste and adjust seasoning if necessary.

Submitted by: Terry Fearon - Cambridge, Ontario, Canada

Butternut Mango Soup

Servings: 6
Proteins/Carbs/Fats: 0 / 1 / 0

Ingredients

3-4 Tbsp Olive Oil, Butter or Ghee

1 Onion (finely chopped)

2 lbs Butternut Squash (peeled and chopped)

2 cups Chicken Broth

2 Very Ripe Mangoes (pureed)

To taste Fresh Coriander (finely chopped)

To taste Unrefined Sea Salt and Pepper

Greek Yogurt

Cinnamon

Directions

Saute onions in oil until soft and almost translucent.

Add chopped butternut and fry for another 5 - 7 minutes.

Add broth and boil for approx 30 minutes till butternut is soft, adding mangoes or mango juice during the last 10 minutes.

Remove from heat and cool down.

Bend in blender till smooth.

Add salt pepper and coriander and reheat before serving.

Dust with cinnamon and add a royal dollop of yogurt just before eating.

Submitted by: Kari - South Africa

Best Ever Butternut Squash Soup

Servings: 8
Proteins/Carbs/Fats: 0 / 1 / 0

Ingredients

1-2 cups Mashed Butternut Squash

2 Red Onions (chopped)

4 stalks Celery (chopped)

1 Banana Pepper (chopped)

2 Carrots (chopped)

3 cups Low Sodium Chicken Stock

1-2 tsp Olive Oil, Butter or Ghee

Directions

In a heavy stock pot, saute onions, pepper, celery and carrots in olive oil until lightly browned.

Cover with chicken stock and simmer 1-2 hours until very soft.

Add in leftover butternut squash and blend using an immersion blender until creamy smooth.

Submitted by: Ellen Jantzen - St. Louis, Missouri

Butternut & Acorn Squash Soup

Servings: 4
Proteins/Carbs/Fats: 0 / 1 / 0

Ingredients

1 Butternut Squash (halved and seeded)

1 Acorn Squash (halved and seeded)

3 Tbsp Butter

1 cup Sweet Onion (chopped)

2-3 cloves Garlic

4 cups Organic Vegetable Broth

1/2 Tsp Ground Black Pepper

1-2 tsp Rosemary

To taste Unrefined Sea Salt

Fresh Jalapeno Pepper (1/4" to 1/2 " slice, seeded)

Directions

Preheat oven to 350º F (175º C).

Place the squash halves cut side down on a parchment-lined cookie sheet. Bake 45 minutes, or until tender. Remove from heat, and cool slightly. Scoop the pulp from the skins. Discard skins.

Melt the butter in a skillet over medium heat, and saute the onion and garlic until tender. Add rosemary.

Blend the squash pulp, onion, broth, pepper, and jalapeno until smooth. This may be done in several batches.

Transfer the soup to a pot over medium heat, and cook, stirring occasionally, until heated through.

Garnish with a dollop of Greek yogurt and seeds from the squash that have been sauteed in butter with a little smoky paprika and honey. Serve warm.

Submitted by: Patty Steffen - Fort Wayne, Indiana

Winter Butternut Squash Soup

Servings: 2
Proteins/Carbs/Fats: 1 / 2 / 0

Ingredients

1 Large Winter Butternut Squash

Olvie Oil

2 Tbsp Butter

1 Tbsp Garlic Rub*

4 oz Greek Yogurt

1 tsp Chicken Base

1 tsp Mushroom Base

1/2 tsp Ground Cinnamon

For Garnish Parsley

***Garlic Rub**

1 clove Garlic or 1/4 tsp Minced in Oil

1/2 Small Onion

1 Tbsp Fresh Parsley or 1 tsp Dried

1 stock Chives (finely cut)

Directions

Cut off the stem of the butternut squash. Cut the entire squash in half, and scoop out the seeds. Grease a jellyroll pan with olive oil; place the two halves of the squash (with skins on), cut side down; bake in a 400º oven for about 30 minutes. Put the cut-up, cooked squash in a pot; add enough water to completely cover the squash (amount needed depends on size of squash, cover with about 1/2 inch more water).

Add butter, garlic rub, Greek yogury, chicken base, mushroom base, and ground cinnamon. Bring the ingredients to a boil, and then turn down the heat to simmer for 30 minutes, or until mushy (garlic and onions are soft).

Let soup cool slightly; then blend until smooth. Spoon into 4-6 bowls and garnsih with parsley.

*To make a thicker soup, add 1 medium potato (peeled, small chunks) to the ingredients in step 2. Make sure to cook them until very soft.

Submitted by: Carolyn Meehan - Cape Cod, MA

Organic Squash & Apple Soup

Servings: 4
Proteins/Carbs/Fats: 0 / 2 / 0

Ingredients

3-4 cups Diced Organic Butternut Squash (cut into 1 inch cubes)

3 cups Macintosh (or any cooking type) Apple (cut into 1 inch cubes)

1 cup Sweet Onion (chopped)

3 cloves Garlic (peeled)

1/4 cup Butter or Olive Oil (or combination of both)

To taste Unrefined Sea Salt, Ground Pepper and Ground Nutmeg

4 cups Vegetable Stock

1/4 cup Plain Yogurt (for garnish)

3 Tbsp Toasted Pumpkin or Sunflower Seeds (for garnish)

1 bunch Chives (finely chopped, for garnish)

Directions

Bake squash, apples, onions, garlic, and butter in a covered dish until soft and mushy, about 20 minutes. Puree in a blender until totally liquid, adding some of the vegetable stock.

In a stock pot, or large pot, combine puree and vegetable stock and bring to a boil. Add the salt, pepper and nutmeg to taste. Adjust seasonings if necessary. You may add more stock or water if you wish, depending on the consistency desired. Pass through a fine mesh strainer and set aside until needed.

Serve topped with plain yogurt, pumpkin seeds and chives.

Submitted by: Marilyn Fisher - Canada

Winter Warmer Butternut Soup

Servings: 2
Proteins/Carbs/Fats: 0 / 2 / 0

Ingredients

1 Butternut Squash

1 Apple

To taste Cinnamon or Nutmeg

To taste Chili or Peppercorns

Coriander Leaves

Directions

Cut the butternut squash length ways and scoop out the seeds. Place on a baking tray face down.

Wash, cut and peel an apple; place it on the baking tray, too.

Bake in the oven for about 30 minutes until tender.

Scoop out the soft, roasted flesh of the squash and put it and the apple in the blender together.

Add the seasoning to taste.

Coriander leaves can be strewn on top to serve.

Enjoy!

The soup is warming and filling as well as naturally thick.

Submitted by: Lindsey Whitehead - Leeds, England

Potato Soups

Curry Sweet Potato Soup

Servings: 8
Proteins/Carbs/Fats: 0 / 2 / 0

Ingredients

1 Tbsp Olive Oil, Butter or Ghee

1 Onion (chopped)

2-4 cloves Garlic (minced)

2-3 Tbsp Curry Powder

3 3/4 cups Chicken Broth

3 cups Water

5-6 Sweet Potatoes (peeled and chopped)

5-6 Carrots (peeled and chopped)

13.5 oz Coconut Milk

Directions

Over medium heat, saute the onion, garlic, and curry powder in olive oil, butter or ghee.

Add broth, water, sweet potatoes, and carrots. Bring to a boil.

Simmer for 20-30 minutes, or until carrots and potatoes are soft.

Use hand blender to puree. Stir in coconut milk. Enjoy!

Another option is to add cinnamon (1 teaspoon). It makes it a whole different flavor, but it's delicious!

Submitted by: Natalie Volkmann - St. Thomas, Ontario

Sweet Potato & Black Bean Chili

Servings: 10
Proteins/Carbs/Fats: 0 / 2 / 0

Ingredients

3 Large Sweet Potatoes (peeled and cut into 1/2" cubes)

1 Large Onion (chopped)

1 Tbsp Olive Oil

2 Tbsp Chili Powder

3 cloves Garlic

1 tsp Ground Cumin

1/4 tsp Cayenne Pepper

2 (15 oz) cans Black Beans (rinsed and drained, ~ 3 1/2 cups)

1 (28 oz) can Diced Tomatoes (with liquid)

1/4 cup Brewed Coffee

2 Tbsp Honey

1/2 tsp Unrefined Sea Salt

1/4 tsp Pepper

1/2 cup Sour Cream (optional)

Cilantro (minced, optional)

Directions

In Dutch oven coated with cooking spray, saute sweet potatoes and onion until crisp tender.

Add the chili powder, garlic, cumin, and cayenne; cook 1 minute longer. Stir in the beans, tomatoes, coffee, honey, salt and pepper.

Bring to a boil. Reduce heat, cover and simmer for 30-35 minutes or until sweet potatoes are tender.

Spoon into bowls and add dollop of sour cream.

Sprinkle with cilantro.

Note: Can add 1 lb chicken cubed and browned with onion and garlic.

Can be done in crockpot on low for 6-8 hours or on high for 4 hours.

Submitted by: Grace - Springboro, OH

Southwestern Sweet Potato Soup

Servings: 6
Proteins/Carbs/Fats: 0 / 1 / 1

Ingredients

1/4 cup Olive Oil, Butter or Ghee

2 Large Onions (peeled and chopped)

4 cloves Garlic (sliced)

4 cups Chicken Broth

2 Large Sweet Potatoes (peeled and grated)

1 Chipotle Pepper (packed in adobo sauce, or any chili pepper if you can't find it)

Garnish:

1 tsp Ground Cinnamon

1 tsp Ground Cumin

1 sprinkle Unrefined Sea Salt

1/2 cup Sour Cream

1 bunch Cilantro (finely minced)

Directions

Using large stockpot, medium-high heat. Add oil and onions. Saute onions until golden brown. Add garlic and cook for a few more minutes.

Pour in the broth and stir in the grated sweet potatoes. Bring to a simmer then add chipotle pepper, cumin, cinnamon, and salt. Continue simmering until potatoes soften.

Carefully puree using a food processer. Taste and add more salt if needed. You can thin the soup by adding 1 cup more water or broth.

As the soup simmers, get the garnish ready. Stir the cilantro into the sour cream. Garnish soup with a dollop of sour cream.

Submitted by: Valerie Moilliet - Canada

Sweet Potato, Chickpea & Spinach Soup

Servings: 6
Proteins/Carbs/Fats: 0 / 1 / 0

Ingredients

2 Tbsp Olive Oil, Butter or Ghee

1 Onion (finely chopped)

1 Large Sweet Potato (peeled and diced)

1 clove Garlic (sliced)

1 tsp Cumin Seed

1 (14 oz) can Chickpeas

2 Tomatoes (roughly chopped)

1 tsp Honey

1 Tbsp Dijon Mustard

1/4 cup Brewed Coffee

3 3/4 cups Hot Vegetable Stock

1 cup Baby Leaf Spinach

Directions

Heat the oil and cook the onion, sweet potato and garlic for 5 minutes, stirring until golden brown.

Add the cumin seeds and cook for 30 seconds.

Stir in the chickpeas, tomatoes, honey and mustard.

Cook for 1 – 2 minutes until the tomatoes begin to soften.

Stir in the hot stock and bring to a boil. Cover and simmer for 10 minutes until the sweet potato is tender.

Stir in the baby leaf spinach and cook for a further minute stirring all the while until the spinach wilts.

*Optional: Puree half of the mixture for a slightly different consistency.

Can serve with homemade spelt bread (shown in photo).

Submitted by: Heather Pendragon - South Eastern Ontario

Judy's Winter Boost Soup

Servings: 6
Proteins/Carbs/Fats: 0 / 2 / 0

Ingredients

1/2 Kabocha Squash (cut into cubes; kabocha is best, but can also use butternut - no need to peel the kabocha)

3-4 Yams (cut into cubes, peeled or not)

4-6 Large Carrots (cut into pennies)

To taste Garlic (chopped or smashed)

To taste Cayenne Pepper

4 cups Chicken Broth (can also use plain water or the leftover water from steaming the veggies)

Extra Virgin Olive Oil

To taste Unrefined Sea SAlt

Greek Yogurt

*Quantities are not as important as making sure there are about equal portions of squash, carrots and yams.

Directions

In a large saucepan, steam squash, carrots, yams and garlic together until tender.

Blend in blender or food processor with chicken broth/ water until soupy. I like mine thick but can thin to taste.

Grate ginger and put into cheesecloth.

Squeeze juice from the ginger pulp into soup.

Discard pulp.

Add salt and cayenne pepper to taste.

Add a small amount of olive oil. Stir well.

Serve with a dollop of yogurt.

Tip: Add leftover fish, shrimp, chicken, turkey and/ or vegetables to individual portions.

Submitted by: Judy Fey

Italian Orange Soup

Servings: 5
Proteins/Carbs/Fats: 0 / 3 / 0

Ingredients

2 Medium Sweet Potatoes

3 Medium Potoates

4 Carrots

1 Butternut Squash

1 Large Onion

3-5 Fresh Garlic Cloves

1-2 Tbsp Olive Oil

Fresh Dill

Frozen or Fresh Pepper

To taste Unrefined Sea Salt and Pepper

Directions

Cut everything into small pieces and add to cold water in a large pot.

Bring to boil and let simmer for half an hour.

Add ginger and dill and cook for another 30 minutes.

Let cool a bit then squash with a food processor.

For fun, leave a few pieces whole.

All done!

Optional: add yogurt when served, and some fresh dill for decoration.

Submitted by: Hadas Noam - Jerusalem, Israel

Allen's Potato Soup

Servings: 6
Proteins/Carbs/Fats: 0 / 1 / 0

Ingredients

4-5 Small Potoates (cut up in bite-size cubes)

1 Small Onion

2 cloves Garlic

1 Roasted Red Pepper

2 Green Onions

3 cups Chicken Stock

3 Tbsp Butter

1/4 cup Milk (optional)

Unrefined Sea Salt & Pepper

For cooking Oil

Directions

Preheat your oven to 400º F.

Roughly chop onion and red pepper; saute in a little oil and butter. After you get a good sizzle, add about 1/2 cup of chicken broth; let simmer until everything is soft and the onions are translucent.

Toss potatoes in oil, salt and pepper; place on a baking sheet in a single layer. Roast potatoes for about 30 minutes, turning once about halfway through. Set aside the equivalent of one potato for later.

By this time the onion, garlic and red pepper should be very soft and cooked down a good bit. Throw in about 3/4 of the finely chopped green onions.

Place the onion and garlic mixture in a blender. Add the potatoes, the rest of the chicken stock, butter and milk (optional). Add salt and pepper as desired.

Pulse the blender until everything is blended (and as smooth or chunky as desired). Pour the whole mixture back in the pot and let it simmer.

Add the potatoes you set aside earlier and serve. Sprinkle green onions on top for garnish.

Submitted by: Allen Cooke

Sweet Potato & Cranberry Soup

Servings: 8
Proteins/Carbs/Fats: 0 / 1 / 0

Ingredients

1 Large Onion (coarsely chopped)

2 Carrots (coarsely chopped)

4 lbs Sweet Potatoes (peeled and cut into 1 inch pieces)

2-3 Tbsp Olive Oil

4 cups Vegetable or Chicken Broth

12-16 oz Prepared Whole Cranberry Sauce

3/4 tsp Ground Nutmeg

1 tsp Ground Ginger

1/2 tsp Ground Cinnamon

1/2 tsp White Pepper

1 tsp Unrefined Sea Salt

Directions

1. Preheat oven to 400ºF. Toss onions, carrots and sweet potatoes in oil and roast them in a large, heavy roasting pan for 45 minutes, stirring occasionally (about every 15 minutes).

2. While vegetables are cooking, puree cranberry sauce in a blender until smooth. Set aside.

3. Place roasted vegetables in a large stockpot. Add broth, nutmeg, ginger, cinnamon, white pepper and salt. Cover and simmer for 15 minutes or until the vegetables are very soft.

4. In a blender or food processor, puree the soup in batches. Add water as needed to achieve desired consistency.

5. Ladle hot soup into individual bowls and drizzle cranberry puree decoratively over the top of each serving.

Submitted by: Ellen Olson

Lentil Soups

Malissa's Winter Lentil Soup

Servings: 6
Proteins/Carbs/Fats: 0 / 2 / 0

Ingredients

4 Leeks (white and light green parts only)

1 bunch Kale

1 Tbsp Olive Oil

1 (28 oz/796mL) can Diced Tomatoes (drained)

6 cups Water

2 Sweet Potatoes (peeled and cut into 1/2 inch dice)

1/2 cup Brown Lentils

1 Tbsp Fresh Thyme Leaves

2 tsp Unrefined Sea Salt

1/4 tsp Black Pepper

Directions

Slice each leek in half lengthwise, then slice each half into half-moons about ¼ inch thick (about 2 cups). Place in a large bowl of cold water and swish to remove any grit. Drain and pat dry.

Remove stems from kale. Stack leaves on top one another and slice crosswise into strips ½ inch wide (about 3 cups).

In a saucepan over medium heat, heat oil. Add leeks and cook for three minutes. Add tomatoes and cook, breaking them up with a spoon, for five minutes. Add water and bring to a boil. Stir in kale, sweet potatoes, lentils, thyme, salt and pepper. Simmer until lentils and sweet potatoes are tender, about 30 - 45 minutes. Spoon into individual bowls.

Submitted by: Malissa Rush - Canada

Karen's Kale & Lentil Soup

Servings: 6
Proteins/Carbs/Fats: 0 / 1 / 0

Ingredients

1 Tbsp Olive Oil, Butter or Ghee

1 Large Onion (minced)

2 stalks Celery (chopped)

2 Large Carrots (chopped)

2-3 cloves Garlic (minced)

3/4 cup Brown and Red Lentils (can use any kind of lentils)

1 Tbsp Tamari

3-4 leafs Kale (washed and cut into thin ribbons)

6 cups Water

To taste Unrefined Sea Salt and Pepper

Directions

Saute the onion, celery, carrots and garlic until tender.

Rinse the lentils and then add to saute mixture with the Tamari and the kale.

Saute all for a few minutes and then add the water and salt and pepper and allow soup to boil on low, covered, for about 45 minutes.

Check the texture of the lentils and cook to your desired taste.

Submitted by: Karen Beagles

Red Lentil Chicken Soup

Servings: 4
Proteins/Carbs/Fats: 2 / 1 / 0

Ingredients

4 cups Chicken Broth

2 cups Water

2 cups Dried Split Red Lentils

1/2 tsp Sea Salt

1 Tbsp Oil (for cooking)

2 Large Boneless Chicken Breasts (cut into 1/2" bits)

1/4 tsp Unrefined Sea Salt

1 cup Minced Onion

1 Tbsp Fresh Grated Ginger Root

1 1/2 tsp Garam Masala

1 (14 oz) can Coconut Milk

1/2 cup Cilantro (minced, optional)

Directions

In large soup pot, over medium high heat, combine the broth, water, lentils, and 1/2 teaspoon salt and bring to a boil.

Reduce heat to medium and cook, covered, about 10 minutes.

In a large saute pan, over medium high heat, heat the oil until it simmers.

Add the chicken and the remaining 1/4 teaspoon salt, stir fry till chicken is getting browned on all sides.

Add the onion, cook 3-5 minutes till the onion has softened.

Add the ginger and garam masala and cook about 1 minute until fragrant.

Add the coconut milk and stir, scraping up any browned bits.

Pour into the broth-lentil mixture and combine.

Reduce heat to medium low and cook for about 15 minutes, until the lentils are tender and the soup has thickened a bit.

Remove from heat and add the cilantro (if using) and black pepper to taste. Makes 6-8 servings.

*This soup tastes even better the next day!

Submitted by: Julie Skinner - Pacific Northwest, USA

Terri's Lentil Soup

Servings: 6
Proteins/Carbs/Fats: 0 / 1 / 0

Ingredients

1 tsp Olive Oil, Butter or Ghee
1 Tbsp Garlic (chopped)
1 Medium Onion (diced)
3 Medium Carrots
16 oz Dried Lentils
8 cups Filtered Water
1 tsp Unrefined Sea Salt
1 tsp Pepper

Directions

In a 6 quart pot, heat the oil on medium heat and sauté the garlic for 1 minute.

Add the onion and continue to sauté until onion has begun to brown stirring frequently.

Rinse and pick through the lentils, removing any stones or twigs.

Add them to the pot.

Stir and add the water.

Cook for approximately 45 minutes to 1 hour or until the lentils are softened.

Add the salt and pepper to taste.

Submitted by: Terri Galindo

Sausage & Lentil Soup with Quinoa & Kale

Servings: 8
Proteins/Carbs/Fats: 1 / 2 / 0

Ingredients

1 Tbsp Olive Oil

1 cup Onion (diced)

1 cup Carrot (diced)

1 cup Celery (diced)

2-3 cloves Garlic (minced)

1 Tbsp Dried Italian Spice Mixture (or the equivalent of thyme, oregano, rosemary)

4 links Any Flavor Chicken or Turkey Sausage (diced)

1 can Petite Diced Tomatoes With Juice (tomatoes with green chiles for some spice)

4-6 cups Organic Chicken Stock (depending on your preference for a thicker or a more broth-y soup)

2 cups Pre-Cooked Lentils

1/2 cup Uncooked Quinoa or 1 cup pre-cooked quinoa

4 cups Chopped Fresh Kale or Spinach (chopped, or cup frozen kael or spinch, chopped)

1 Tbsp Balsamic Vinegar (optional)

To taste Unrefined Sea Salt & Pepper

Raw-Milk Parmesan Cheese (optional)

Directions

Dice onion, carrot and celery. Heat olive oil in stockpot. Add veggies and saute until starting to soften, about 3-4 minutes. Add garlic and Italian seasoning; saute about 2 minutes more.

Add canned tomatoes, chicken stock, cooked lentils, and quinoa to pot, and cook on high until boiling. Turn down to simmer, and cover with lid. Cook for 10-15 minutes until quinoa is starting to show its "curlicues" (individual grains will be somewhat translucent, with an opaque rim around the outside when cooked.) Remove cover and add sausage, continuing to simmer for 5-10 minutes or until sausage is heated through.

Five minutes before serving, add chopped kale or spinach and cook until wilted. Season with salt, pepper and balsamic vinegar, if desired. Serve hot, with Parmesan cheese sprinkled on top.

Submitted by: Jan

Greek Red Lentil Soup

Servings: 4
Proteins/Carbs/Fats: 0 / 1 / 1

Ingredients

2 cups Red Lentils

2 Tbsp Oil

1 Large Yellow Onion (diced)

2 tsp Unrefined Sea Salt

8 cloves Garlic (minced)

2 Carrots (diced)

1 tsp Cracked Pepper

1/4 tsp Red Chile Flakes

1 Tbsp Minced Rosemary

2 Tbsp Minced Oregano

2 Bay Leaves

8 cups Vegetable Stock

1/2 Lemon (zested)

2 Lemons (juiced)

1 cup Crumbled Feta Cheese (optional)

2 tsp Minced Rosemary

Directions

Rinse lentils; drain.

Saute oil, onion and 1 teaspoon of salt.

Add garlic, carrot, and spices (except for rosemary).

Cook over medium heat just until carrots are tender.

Add lentils and vegetable stock, bring to a boil.

Reduce heat and partially cover. Cook until lentils are soft and fall apart.

Season with lemon zest and juice, salt, pepper and rosemary, (and optional feta cheese), and serve.

Submitted by: Andra Rempel

Simple Delicious Lentil Soup

Servings: 8
Proteins/Carbs/Fats: 0 / 1 / 0

Ingredients

5 cups Water

1 cup Dry Lentils

1 Medium Onion (cut into small pieces)

1 Large Carrot (sliced thinly)

1 Large Stalk Celery (slivered)

1 (15 oz) can Tomato Sauce

Directions

Pour lentils into water. Bring to boil and, while cooking, prepare the remaining ingredients.

Saute onion briefly in a small amount of oil or butter. Add carrot and celery, and saute together for a couple minutes.

Add onion, carrot and celery to the lentils, which by now are nearly cooked. Continue cooking 5-10 minutes, or until veggies are your style of consistency. (Lentils take only about 30 minutes cooking time.)

Add tomato sauce, plus enough water to rinse the can.

Heat through and serve.

Submitted by: JoAn Witzel - Ridgecrest, California

Healthy & Hearty Lentil Vegetable Soup

Servings: 8
Proteins/Carbs/Fats: 0 / 1 / 0

Ingredients

2 cups Red Lentils

4 quarts Water

1 Bay Leaf

1 Tbsp Olive Oil, Butter or Ghee

1 White Onion (diced)

1 cup Carrots (sliced)

5 cloves Garlic (minced)

1 Sweet Potato (diced)

1 cup Celery (chopped)

1 Red Bell Pepper (diced)

1 Tbsp Ground Cumin

3 tsp Unrefined Sea Salt (or to taste)

1 tsp White Pepper

1/4 cup Fresh Parsley (chopped)

Directions

If making on the stovetop:

Boil lentils and bay leaf in water until lentils are soft.

Heat oil on medium-high heat.

Add garlic and saute until golden.

Add onions, celery, and bell pepper. Saute until tender.

Add onion/celery/bell pepper/ garlic mixture to lentils and water.

Add potato and carrot.

Cover and simmer for 30 minutes.

Add chopped parsley, salt and pepper. Simmer for 10 minutes more.

Garnish with chopped green onions and/or parmesan cheese, if desired.

If making in the slowcooker:

Add lentils, bay leaf and water to slowcooker. Cover and turn on high while you prepare other ingredients.

Complete steps 2-6 above.

Lower setting on slowcooker to low and cook for 8 hours or keep on high and cook for 4 hours.

One hour before done in slowcooker, complete steps 8 and 9 above.

Submitted by: Kendra Good - Wyoming

Wanda's Steak Soup

Servings: 6
Proteins/Carbs/Fats: 5 / 1 / 0

Ingredients

2 lbs Beef (trimmed and cut into 1 inch cubes)

1/2 cup Onion (diced)

1 Small Jalapeno (seeded and diced small, optional)

2 Tbsp Olive Oil, Butter or Ghee

6 cups Beef Stock

1 (15 oz) can Crushed Tomatoes

1/2 cup Carrots (diced into 1 inch pieces)

1 cup Peas

1 cup Green Beans (diced into 1 inch pieces)

1 cup Gold Baby Potatoes (diced into 1 inch pieces)

1/2 cup Lentils

Directions

Generously season beef cubes with onion powder, garlic powder, celery seed, black pepper and sea salt.

Heat two tablespoons of oil in a large pot.

When very hot, add seasoned beef and sear on all sides.

After the first time you stir the beef, add the onion.

If you like a bit of spice, add the jalapeno.

Cook until onion is transparent.

Add beef stock and crushed tomatoes.

Bring to a boil.

Reduce heat and simmer on low for about 1 hour.

Taste soup for seasoning and adjust according to taste.

Add all the vegetables and the lentils.

Bring to boil, reduce to simmer and cook for 45 minutes to 1 hour longer.

Serve.

Submitted by: Wanda Schartman - St. Louis, Missouri

Spanish Soups

Mexican Chicken Posole Soup

Servings: 8
Proteins/Carbs/Fats: 1 / 2 / 0

Ingredients

1 Tbsp Olive Oil, Butter or Ghee

1 Large Chicken Breast (diced)

1 Medium Onion (chopped)

4 cloves Garlic (minced)

1 Jalapeno (minced, optional)

1 (29 oz) can Diced Tomatoes with Juice

1 (32 oz) can Chicken Broth

4 cups Quinoa

1 (4 oz) can Chopped Mild Green Chiles

1 tsp Unrefined Sea Salt

1 tsp Oregano

1 tsp Cumin

1/4 tsp Cayenne Pepper

Greek Yogurt

5 sprigs Cilantro (chopped)

Directions

In a soup pot, saute the chicken with oil, onion, garlic and jalapeno until the chicken is done and onion is soft.

Add diced tomatoes, chicken broth, quinoa, green chiles, sea salt, oregano, cumin and pepper. Simmer.

Simmer 20 minutes to blend flavors. This is thick like stew, so you may want to add more broth.

Ladle soup into bowls. Garnish with a dollop of Greek yogurt and some cilantro.

Submitted by: PJ - Colorado

Larry's Tortilla Soup

Servings: 8
Proteins/Carbs/Fats: 4 / 1 / 1

Ingredients

Rotisserie Chicken

1 Medium Onion

1 Jalapeno

1 cup Carrots (chopped)

1 1/2 cups Celery (chopped)

1/2 bunch Cilantro

6 1/2 cups Organic Chicken Broth

1 1/4 cups Water

2 cups Shredded Cheese (optional)

1 Avocado (sliced)

1 Tbsp Pinto Bean Seasoning

1 Tbsp Cumin

2 Tbsp Olive Oil, Butter or Ghee

Directions

De-bone and shred chicken.

Finely dice onion and jalapeno and sauté in large pot. Keep stirring until onions are translucent.

Add chicken broth and water and bring to a boil.

Add carrots and celery. Lower heat and simmer until carrots and celery are soft (about 10 minutes).

Add shredded chicken.

Add cumin and pinto bean seasoning.

Simmer for 20 minutes.

Fill bowl with soup; add cheese (optional), cilantro, and avocado.

Salt and pepper to taste.

Submitted by: Larry Felix

Crockpot Taco Soup

Servings: 8
Proteins/Carbs/Fats: 2 / 1 / 0

Ingredients

2-3 Free Range Chicken Breasts (about 1 lb)

2 Tbsp Olive Oil

3-4 Smaller Organic Leeks (chopped)

3 cloves Organic Garlic (minced)

2 Tbsp Isabel's Taco Seasoning

28 oz Organic Fire Roasted Diced Tomatoes (use 1 1/2 cans if you double)

1 (4 oz) can Diced Green Chiles

1 oz Diced Jalapeno Peppers

8 oz Aribba Chili Sauce - Mild (special ingredient - it is with the salsa)

1 can Organic Black Beans

1 Can Organic Pinto Beans

Directions

Slice the chicken breasts into strips and cook in 1 tablespoon of olive oil.

Once chicken is fully cooked, sauté with 1 more tablespoon of olive oil, chopped leeks and garlic.

Let cool and dice chicken.

Place all ingredients into a crock pot except cheese.

Cook on low for 6 hours or high for 4.

It is even better heated up and it freezes great.

Isabel's DIY Taco Seasoning

6 Tbsp Chili Powder

2 Tbsp Cumin

4 Tbsp Paprika

3 Tbsp Onion Powder

1 Tbsp Garlic Powder

1 tsp Cayenne Pepper

Submitted by: Patty Boone - Hillsboro, Tennessee

Caldo Verde

Servings: 10
Proteins/Carbs/Fats: 1 / 1 / 0

Ingredients

1 Tbsp Olive Oil, Butter or Ghee

1 Onion

1 Large Stalk Celery with Leaves

3 cloves Garlic

4-6 Chorizo-style Turkey Sausages

6 cups Chicken Broth

1 Large Head of Cauliflower

6 cups Kale (washed and chopped)

To taste Unrefined Sea Salt and Pepper

Directions

Chop the onion, garlic and celery.

Heat the oil on medium heat in a large pot and saute them.

Squeeze the chorizo out of its casing into the pot and break up the meat into small lumps with a wooden spoon. Cook while stirring for about 10 minutes.

When the vegetables are translucent and the meat is cooked add the chicken broth and the cauliflower and bring to a boil.

Cover the pot and reduce heat to a low simmer for about 15 minutes (until the cauliflower is very soft).

Puree the soup right in the pot with a wand mixer (or in batches in a blender or food processor).

When smooth add the chopped kale and simmer for 6-8 minutes. Add salt and pepper to taste.

Enjoy.

Submitted by: Carol Kushner

Hot Taco Soup

Servings: 8
Proteins/Carbs/Fats: 3 / 1 / 0

Ingredients

1 1/2 lbs Ground Bison (organic, grass-fed)

1 Medium Onion (chopped)

2 stalks Celery (chopped)

1 (17 oz) can Diced Tomatoes with Juice

2 (14 oz) cans Kidney Beans (or your favorite kind)

1 (8 oz) package Frozen Corn

1 package Taco Seasoning (see bottom of page for homemade seasoning)

1 tsp Garlic Powder

1 tsp Chili Powder

1 cup Organic Chicken Broth

Optional Garnish: Diced Avocado, Sliced Green Onion or Fresh Cilantro

Directions

In large stockpot, brown ground bison, onion and celery.

Drain grease, add tomatoes & all ingredients but garnish.

Simmer for at least 30 minutes.

Serve in individual bowls and garnish as desired.

Taco Seasoning

1 Tbsp Chili Powder

1/4 tsp Garlic Powder

1/4 tsp Onion Powder

1/4 tsp Crushed Red Pepper Flakes

1/4 tsp Oregano

1/2 tsp Paprika

1 1/2 tsp Cumin

1 tsp Unrefined Sea Salt

1 tsp Black Pepper

Submitted by: Lori Case

Tortilla-less Soup

Servings: 4
Proteins/Carbs/Fats: 4 / 1 / 1

Ingredients

2-3 Large Boneless, Skinless Chicken Breasts

2 cups Beef Broth

2 cups Chicken Broth

2 cups Water

1 cup Diced Tomatoes or 1 (14.5 oz) can Diced Tomatoes

1/4 cup Chopped Green Pepper

1 cup Sliced Carrots

1/2 cup Chopped Onion

1 cup Fresh Whole Kernel Corn (or use frozen)

1 (15 oz) can Black Beans (drained and rinsed)

1 tsp Chili Powder

1/4 tsp Black Pepper

1 tsp Ground Cumin

1 Avocado (peeled and chopped)

Snipped Fresh Cilantro

Lime Wedges

Directions

Cut chicken into 1 inch cubes & set aside.

In a large soup pan, combine water, beef, & chicken broth, undrained tomatoes, onion, carrots and green pepper.

Bring to a gentle boil.

Reduce heat and add chicken, corn, chili powder, cumin and black pepper.

Cover and simmer at least 30 minutes, but longer is fine.

To serve, ladle soup into bowls and sprinkle with avocado and cilantro.

Provide lime wedges for individuals to squeeze into their own bowl.

* Increase or decrease the liquids depending on how robust you want the soup to be (you may need to add a dash or two of salt).

*A variety of fresh vegetables can be added, such as squash, zucchini, cabbage, spinach, mushrooms, etc., for a different variation.

Submitted by: Kathy Buckmaster - Wake Forest, NC

Puchero

Servings: 6
Proteins/Carbs/Fats: 3 / 1 / 0

Ingredients

3 lbs Shin Meat with Marrow Bone (chicken, can use cut-up stewing hen or cubed pork butt instead)

6 cloves Garlic

2 Tbsp Ground Cumin

1 1/2 Tbsp Unrefined Sea Salt

1 tsp Pepper

1/4 tsp Ground Cloves

3 Zucchini (peeled and chopped in 1 1/2" pieces)

1 Peeled Ripe (black) Plaintain (chopped in 1 1/2" pieces)

1 Chayote (cut into 1 1/2" cubes)

4 Large Carrots (cut in 1 1/2" pieces)

2 Sweet Potatoes or Yams (peeled and in 1 1/2" cubes)

3" Pieces of Corn on the Cob

Garnish: Diced Radish, Cilantro Leaves, Diced Onion, Lemon or Lime Wedges, Cayenne Pepper

Submitted by: Susan Gomez-Baer

Directions

Broth: Put water on to boil. Cut the membrane surrounding the shin meat in a couple of places so it doesn't curl up when cooking. Put the meat into the pot once the water boils; wait until it's boiling again and let boil for 5 minutes, then drain the water. Rinse the meat. Put the parboiled meat into the same pot or a pressure cooker, with cold water to cover by 2 inches. Add the salt, pepper, garlic, cloves, and cumin. Put the heat on high. Once the water boils, turn the heat down to a simmer and cook for 2.5 hours. Add water if needed. (For a pressure cooker, cook 1.5 hours at a low hiss.) Turn the heat off and let the meat cool in the broth until it is just warm enough to eat. Put the meat on a serving plate.

Vegetables: Put the carrots and potatoes in salted boiling water, and cook them at a medium boil for 5 minutes. Add the corn, and continue cooking for 5 minutes. Add the chayote and cook once the water boils again for 3 minutes. Then add the plaintain, and zucchini. Cook for 5 minutes or until the zucchini are cooked to your taste. Drain the vegetables and put them into a serving bowl.
To serve: The meat and vegetables are served in the broth or on the side. Add the garnish to taste for a contrast of flavor and texture.

Malena's Taco Soup

Servings: 6
Proteins/Carbs/Fats: 4 / 2 / 0

Ingredients

1 1/2 lbs Ground Turkey

1 Medium Onion

1 package Taco Seasoning

2 (16 oz) cans Pinto Beans

1 (16 oz) can Kidney Beans

1 (14.5 oz) can Chili Beans

1 (11 oz) can Corn

1 (16 oz) can Tomato Sauce

1 (26 oz) can Chopped Tomatoes

3 cups Water

1 Green Pepper (diced)

Directions

Brown ground turkey with onion in pan.

Drain and add taco seasoning, beans, corn, tomato sauce and chopped tomatoes.

Add 3 cups water. Bring to boil and let simmer.

Add diced green pepper about 15 minutes before serving.

This can be cooked in a crock pot on low for 6-8 hours.

Submitted by: Malena Ogden

Jean's Tortilla Soup

Servings: 8
Proteins/Carbs/Fats: 3 / 1 / 0

Ingredients

1-2 lbs Ground Turkey (or any other ground meat of your choice, browned)

1 Onion (chopped)

3 Tbsp Minced Garlic

1 Tbsp Chili Powder

1 1/2 tsp Dried Oregano

1 Tbsp Paprika

1 Tbsp Cumin

1 tsp Crushed Red Pepper Flakes (more or less depending on how hot you like it)

1 (28 oz) can Diced Tomatoes with Liquid

1 1/2 cups Chicken Broth

1 (11 oz) can Whole Corn with Liquid

1 (14.5 oz) can Black Beans with Liquid

1 (4 oz) can Chopped Green Chiles with Liquid

1/4 cup Cilantro (chopped)

Directions

Put all the ingredients in a large crock pot and cook for several hours on high until onions are soft.

Garnish with chopped avocado and chopped green onions.

Submitted by: Jean Baraghoshi - Salt Lake City, Utah

Spicy Calorie-Burning Mexican Soup

Servings: 8
Proteins/Carbs/Fats: 1 / 1 / 0

Ingredients

2 Tbsp Olive Oil, Butter or Ghee

1 tsp Unrefined Sea Salt

3 cloves Garlic

1 Yellow Bell Pepper

1 Fresh Jalapeno Pepper (chopped)

1 (4 oz) can Chopped Green Chiles

1 (16 oz) can Petite Diced Tomatoes

2 cups Frozen Corn

1 (6 oz) can Tomato Paste

1 large box Chicken Broth

1 bunch Cilantro (chopped)

1 Tbsp Cumin

1 tsp Coriander

2 Dried Habenero Peppers

1 can Black Beans (rinsed and drained)

2 Chicken Breasts (with or without ribs, shred after tenderly cooked)

Directions

Sauté oil, salt, garlic, yellow pepper, jalapeno pepper and onion in Dutch oven.

Add remaining ingredients, and simmer on medium low heat for 3 hours.

Optional: Top with small amount of favorite cheese.

Submitted by: Tammy Colvocoresses - Lone Tree, CO

Brazilian Coconut Soup

Servings: 8
Proteins/Carbs/Fats: 2 / 1 / 0

Ingredients

2 Tbsp Olive Oil

1 Onion (chopped)

1 Green Bell Pepper (chopped)

3 cloves Garlic (minced)

1 (16 oz) can Diced Tomatoes (drained)

3/4 cup Long-Grain Brown Rice

1/4 tsp Red Pepper Flakes

1 3/4 tsp Celtic Sea Salt

3 cups Chicken Stock

2 cups Water

1 cup Canned Unsweetened Coconut Milk

1 lb Cooked Chicken Breast (cut into strips)

1/4 tsp Fresh-Ground Black Pepper

2 Tbsp Fresh Lime Juice

1/2 cup Chopped Fresh Cilantro

Directions

In a large pot, heat the oil over moderately low heat. Add the onion, bell pepper, and garlic and cook, stirring occasionally, until the vegetables start to soften, about 10 minutes.

Add the rice, red-pepper flakes, salt, tomatoes, and water to the pot. Bring to a boil and cook until the rice is almost tender, about 10 minutes.

Stir the coconut milk into the soup. Bring back to a simmer and then stir in the chicken. Simmer, stirring occasionally, until warmed through 3-5 minutes. Stir in the black pepper, lime juice, and cilantro.

Could also be prepared with shrimp instead of chicken.

*Inspired by a soup served at Villa Montez restaurant in Tyler, Texas.

Submitted by: Malissa Rush - Dallas, Texas

South of the Border Soup with Avocado Pico de Gallo

Servings: 8
Proteins/Carbs/Fats: 0 / 1 / 0

Ingredients

3 ears Roasted or Boiled Corn on the Cob

1/2 tsp Olive Oil

To taste Unrefined Sea Salt and Black Pepper

1 slice Bacon (cut crosswise into 3/8 inch strips)

1 Medium Size Red Onion (chopped)

6 cloves Garlic (finely minced)

1 Bay Leaf (crumbled)

5 cups Defatted Chicken Stock

4 sprigs Cilantro

Avocado Pico de Gallo

3 Roma Tomatoes (cored and seeded)

1 Serrano Chili (stem, vein and seeds removed)

4 Tbsp Cilantro Leaves (roughly chopped)

3/4 tsp Salt

1 tsp Black Pepper

1 Avocado (cut into 1 1/4" pieces)

1 Tbsp Fresh Lime Juice

Directions

Preheat oven to 350° F and prepare grill. Rub corn lightly with oil, then season with salt and pepper. Cook on grill for 10 minutes, turning once. (Alternatively, corn may be broiled.) Remove corn from grill. Stand each ear of corn on end and remove kernels with a chef's knife. Reserve kernels and cobs separately.

Place bacon in soup pot over medium-high heat. Cook until almost crisp, then discard fat. Add onion to pot and cook until translucent. Add garlic and cook until mixture begins to brown. Add bay leaf and stock, then bring to a boil. Stir in reserved corn cobs and reduce heat to a simmer; cook 25 minutes.

Prepare Avocado Pico de Gallo: Dice tomatoes into 3/8-inch cubes and transfer to a medium –size bowl. Mince serrano chili and add to tomatoes, along with cilantro, salt, pepper, avocado and lime juice; toss well to combine.

When broth mixture is done, remove corn cobs with tongs. Stir reserved corn kernels into soup and heat through. Stir in pico de gallo, then taste and correct seasoning. Ladle soup into bowls and top with cilantro sprigs.

Submitted by: Marlene Ditmore - Conroe, Texas

Bolivian Oatmeal Soup

Servings: 4
Proteins/Carbs/Fats: 2 / 1 / 0

Ingredients

1 quart to 6 cups Water (for beef) or Organic Chicken Broth (for chicken)

To taste Unrefined Sea Salt

1/2 lb Bone-in Beef (without fat) or Chicken

1/4 cup Carrots (cut in small squares)

1/4 cup Onion (finely chopped)

1/4 cup Fresh Tomato (cut in small pieces)

1/2 cup (or more) Potatoes (peeled, sliced 1/4 inch thick, and cut in 1" squares)

1/4 cup Old Fashioned Oats (toasted, directions to right)

2-4 Tbsp Fresh or Frozen Peas

1/4 - 1/2 tsp Crushed Dry Oregano

Directions

Bring liquid to a boil first, then add salt and meat (either beef OR chicken). Add all the vegetables except the potatoes and peas. Cover and let boil for 30 minutes on low heat until very tender and onion nearly disappears. Then remove meat and cut into small pieces. Return meat without bone to pot. Add potatoes and boil on low until almost cooked.

Directions for toasting oats: Heat frying pan on medium heat. Do not add oil. Toast raw oats for about 3 minutes until lightly brown, tossing constantly. (They may make a faint crackling sound.)

Add toasted oats and peas to boiling soup and boil with lid tipped for 3 to 5 minutes more until tender, but not "mushy."

When soup is done, add the oregano. Serve and enjoy.

Sudmitted by: Marilyn Sheldahl

Bean Soups

White Bean & Chicken Chili

Servings: 3
Proteins/Carbs/Fats: 3 / 1 / 0

Ingredients

For cooking Butter

1 Large Onion (chopped)

4 cloves Garlic (minced)

2 lbs Ground Chicken

1 tsp Unrefined Sea Salt (plus more for seasoning)

2 Tbsp Ground Cumin

2 Tbsp Fennel Seeds

1 Tbsp Dried Oregano

2 Tbsp Chili Powder

3 Tbsp Coconut Flour or Rice Four

2 (15 oz) cans Cannellini or Other White Beans (rinsed and drained)

1 bunch Swiss Chard (about 1 lb, stems removed, leaves chopped into 1" pieces)

4 cups Low-Sodium Chicken Stock

1/4 tsp Crushed Red Pepper Flakes

To taste Freshly Ground Black Pepper

1/4 cup Fresh-Leaf Parsley (chopped)

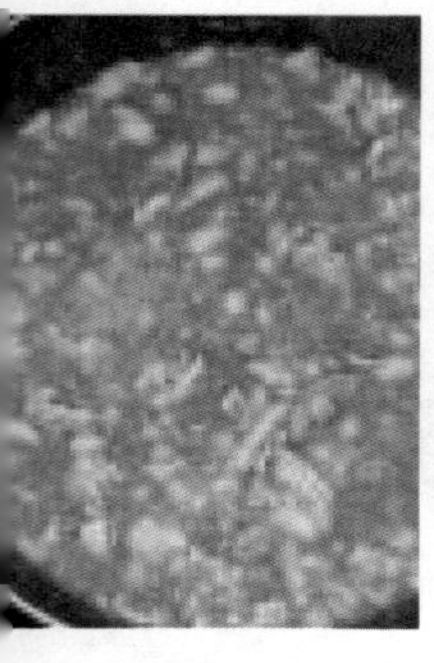

Directions

In a large heavy-bottomed saucepan or Dutch oven, heat the butter over medium-high heat. Add the onion and cook until translucent, about 5 minutes. Add the garlic and cook for 30 seconds.

Add the ground chicken, 1 teaspoon salt, cumin, fennel seeds, oregano, and chili powder. Cook, stirring frequently, until the chicken is cooked through, about 8 minutes.

Stir the flour into the chicken mixture. Add the beans, Swiss chard, and chicken stock. Bring the mixture to simmer, scraping up the brown bits that cling to the bottom of the pan with a wooden spoon.

Simmer for 55-60 minutes until the liquid has reduced by about half and the chili has thickened. Add the red pepper flakes and simmer for another 10 minutes. Season with salt and pepper, to taste.

Ladle the chili into serving bowls. Sprinkle with chopped parsley.

Submitted by: Dawn Wilson - Jefferson City, Missouri

BBQ Ribs & Bean Soup

Servings: 6
Proteins/Carbs/Fats: 5 / 1 / 0

Ingredients

1 (16 oz) package Great Northern Beans

3/4 cup Onion (chopped)

1/8 tsp Pepper

2 lbs Beef Short Ribs (cut into serving-size pieces)

6 cups Water

1 cup Barbecue Sauce

1-2 tsp Unrefined Sea Salt

Directions

Cover beans with water in a large soup pot; soak overnight. Drain.

Combine beans, onion, pepper and short ribs in a slow cooker; add enough water to cover. Cover and cook on low setting for 10-12 hours.

Remove short ribs; cut meat from bones. Return meat to slow cooker; stir in sauce and salt to taste. Cover and cook on high setting for an additional 20 minutes, until warmed through.

Submitted by: Jim & Patt Johnsen - Alexandria,Minnesota

Moroccan Chickpea Stew

Servings: 12
Proteins/Carbs/Fats: 0 / 1 / 0

Ingredients

Olive Oil, Butter or Ghee

1 cup Onions (chopped)

1/2 cup Celery (diced)

1/2 cup Red Pepper (chopped)

1 cup Zucchini and/or Eggplant (diced)

1 clove Garlic (minced)

3 cups Vegetable Broth (low sodium preferred)

3 cups Sweet Potatoes (cubed)

1 (19 oz) can Diced Tomatoes

1 Tbsp Lemon Juice

2 tsp Gingerroot (grated)

1 tsp Ground Cumin

1 tsp Curry Powder

1 tsp Ground Coriander

1 tsp Chili Powder

1/4 tsp Black Pepper

1/2 cup Raisins

2 Tbsp Natural Peanut Butter

2 Tbsp Fresh Cilantro (chopped)

Directions

Heat butter or olive oil in a large, non-stick saucepan over medium-high heat. Add onions, celery, green pepper, zucchini, eggplant and garlic. Cook and stir until vegetables begin to soften, about 3 minutes.

Add remaining ingredients, except raisins, peanut butter and cilantro. Bring to a boil. Reduce heat to low and simmer, covered, for 20 minutes.

Stir in raisins, peanut butter, and cilantro. Mix well. Simmer for 5 minutes. Serve hot.

Submitted by: Janet - Vancouver, British Columbia

Tuscan Tuna & Cannellini Beans

Servings: 8
Proteins/Carbs/Fats: 2 / 1 / 0

Ingredients

1/3 cup Fresh Squeezed Orange Juice

1 Onion (chopped)

2/3 cup Dry Vermouth or Dry White Wine

1/4 cup White Wine Vinegar

1 lb Fresh Tuna Steaks (cut into 1-inch cubes)

4 cups Cooked Cannellini Beans or Canned Cannellini Beans (rinsed and drained)

2 Tomatoes (coarsely chopped)

1/4 cup Fresh Basil (chopped)

1/2 tsp Ground Pepper

2 Tbsp Grated Orange Zest

1 Tbsp Chopped Chives

Directions

In a large nonstick frying pan over medium-high heat, heat the orange juice. Add the onion and sauté until wilted, about 5 minutes. Add the vermouth or wine and vinegar and continue to sauté for 2 minutes.

Reduce heat to medium and stir in the fish, beans, tomatoes, basil, pepper, and half of the orange zest. Cover and cook until the fish is opaque throughout, 7-9 minutes.

To serve, divide among individual plates. Sprinkle with the chives and remaining orange zest.

Submitted by Rachel - Lincoln, Nebraska

Fifteen Bean Soup

Servings: 16
Proteins/Carbs/Fats: 1 / 1 / 0

Ingredients

1 (20 oz) bag 15 Bean Mix with Seasoning Packet

1 lb Ham Steaks (cubed, or about 2 cups cubed chicken breast)

2 (14.5 oz) cans Chicken Broth

1 quart Water

1 (28 oz) can Diced Tomatoes

2 Tbsp Olive Oil, Butter or Ghee

2 cloves Garlic (minced)

1 cup Sweet Onion (chopped)

1 cup Celery (chopped)

1 cup Carrots (quartered and finely sliced)

1/2 cup Medium Thick and Chunky Salsa

1 Tbsp Lemon Juice

To taste Unrefined Sea Salt and Pepper

Directions

Prepare Beans: Sort out any bad beans or foreign particles – wash in cold water – place in large pot and cover with 2 ½ quarts water. Bring to a boil for 2 minutes, remove from heat and soak in covered pot for 1 hour. Discard soaking water and rinse the beans off.

Prepare Soup: Put prepared beans in large pot and add chicken broth, water, and ham (or chicken). Cover and bring to a boil – reduce heat and simmer about an hour or until beans are tender.

Saute garlic, onion, celery and carrots in oil for about 10 minutes. Add sautéed veggies, salsa, lemon juice, seasoning packet (from bean mix) and salt and pepper to taste to the bean mixture. Simmer an additional 20-30 minutes until veggies are tender.

Submitted by: Cathy Cherpes

Curried Tomato & White Bean Soup

Servings: 8
Proteins/Carbs/Fats: 0 / 1 / 0

Ingredients

1 Tbsp Olive Oil, Butter or Ghee

1 Medium Onion (chopped)

1 Tbsp Curry Powder

3/4 tsp Ground Ginger

2 (15 oz) cans Cannelli Beans (drained and rinsed)

1 (28 oz) can Diced Tomatoes (undrained)

1 3/4 cups Water

Directions

Heat a large saucepan over medium heat until hot. Add oil and onions; cook for 5 minutes or until onions are translucent.

Stir in curry and ginger and cook very briefly. Stir in beans, tomatoes and water. Bring to a boil. Reduce heat and simmer for 15 minutes.

Submitted by: Leigh Hottel - North Myrtle Beach, SC

Funky 15 Bean Soup

Servings: 12
Proteins/Carbs/Fats: 3 / 1 / 0

Ingredients

1 (16 oz) package 15 Different Kinds of Beans

6 (28 oz each) boxes Beef Stock

5 Broccoli Stems

2 Large Onions

1/2 lb Sausage*

4 Parsnips

5 Carrots

1 cup Celery

26 oz (or 3 cups) Pork

Tarragon

Black Pepper

Italian Seasoning Blend

Garlic Powder

*Soup pictured used Cajun Style Andouille Sausage

*Can also use chicken

Directions

Soak package of beans in boiling water for one hour. Rinse. Add two more cups of water and six boxes of beef stock.

Chop the broccoli stems, onions, sausage, parsnips, carrots, celery and pork. Add to the pot (may require two pots).

Season with tarragon, black pepper, Italian seasoning blend and garlic powder. Simmer for several hours.

Submitted by: Dianne Lambart - Michigan

Chupe with Cannellini Beans

Servings: 8
Proteins/Carbs/Fats: 0 / 1 / 0

Ingredients

2 slices Back Bacon (chopped)

2 cloves Garlic (finely chopped)

2 Celery Sticks (finely chopped)

1 Leek (cut in rings)

1 Large or 2 Smaller Carrots (chopped)

1 Red Pepper (chopped)

1 Medium Parsnip (chopped, optional)

1 Potato (peeled and chopped into cubes)

1 (10.5 oz) can Cannellini Beans (drained and rinsed)

40 oz Chicken or Vegetable Stock (homemade)

1 tsp Italian Dried Herbs

1 pinch Black Pepper

Oil

Fresh Cilantro

Directions

Place first seven ingredients in large saucepan with oil.

Cook gently about five minutes, stirring around a bit.

Season with Italian herbs and pepper.

Add potato, beans and stock.

Simmer gently for about half an hour.

Leave to stand an hour or 2 if you can - not essential but improves flavour.

Reheat.

Put coriander leaves in bottom of soup bowls, and ladle soup over; or scatter coriander over top as garnish.

Submitted by: Patricia - United Kingdom

Beef & Navy Bean Soup

Servings: 3
Proteins/Carbs/Fats: 3 / 1 / 0

Ingredients

1 Large Onion (cubed)

2 Large Carrots (sliced chunky)

2 Large Stocks Celery (sliced chunky)

3 cloves Garlic (minced)

1 lb Stew Beef (sliced into small bites)

1 Tbsp Olive Oil

1 tsp Butter

1 can Consume or Beef Broth

1 can Navy Beans

Directions

Melt butter and olive oil in pan.

Brown the beef; when it is almost browned add the onions, carrots, celery, garlic.

Saute until they are tender (about 2 more minutes).

Pour in the consume or beef broth (consume gives a much deeper finished taste), the can of beans (drained first) and add a quart of water or so to the pot.

Let the whole thing simmer for a couple hours.

Submitted by: Jill Hart

Zucchini Chili

Servings: 8
Proteins/Carbs/Fats: 2 / 2 / 0

Ingredients

1 Large Diced Purple Onion

1 Large Zucchini (cut into 1/2 inch cubes)

2-4 cloves Garlic (minced)

1 lb Grass-Fed Beef or Free-Range Ground Turkey Breast

1 (15 oz) can Black Beans (drained and rinsed)

1 (15 oz) can Red Kidney Beans (drained and rinsed)

5-10 Tomatoes (or two 15 oz cans diced tomatoes)

2-3 Tbsp Chili Seasoning

Directions

Sauté first three ingredients in olive oil in a large stock-pot over medium-high heat about 5 minutes (or until tender). Stir in beef and continue sautéing until beef is lightly browned. Add remaining ingredients and bring to boil. Reduce heat and simmer uncovered about 20 minutes, stirring often.

NOTE: May add diced bell pepper with the first three ingredients; may serve with brown or black rice or quinoa to reduce sharpness of chili; and may be frozen up to 3 months.

Submitted by: Steph Rieffanaugh

Vegetable Chili

Servings: 20
Proteins/Carbs/Fats: 0 / 1 / 0

Ingredients

1 cup Onions (chopped)

1 cup Carrots (chopped)

2 cloves Garlic (minced)

1 cup Green Bell Pepper (chopped)

1 cup Turnips (chopped)

1 Zucchini (chopped)

1 cup Celery (chopped)

2 Tbsp Chili Powder

1 package Fresh Mushrooms (chopped)

2 (28 oz) cans Whole Peeled Tomatoes with liquid (chopped)

1 (15 oz) can Kidney Beans (drained and rinsed)

1 (15 oz) can Black Beans (drained and rinsed)

1 Tbsp Ground Cumin

To taste Red Pepper Flakes

1-2 boxes Chicken Stock (depending on how many vegetables you have)

Directions

Combine all ingredients in a large pot.

Cook until vegetables are tender.

Optional:

Garnish bowls with fresh salsa and cilantro.

Add ground beef.

Submitted by: Dianne Lambert - Michigan

Lisa's Autumn Harvest Soup

Servings: 15
Proteins/Carbs/Fats: 0 / 1 / 0

Ingredients

2 Red Peppers (roasted, skin removed after)

3 Tbsp Olive Oil

1 cup Onion (chopped)

2 tsp Cumin

1 tsp Crushed Red Pepper Flakes

1 tsp Paprika

1/2 tsp Unrefined Sea Salt

4 cloves Garlic (sliced thin, using a razor blade works very well)

2 cups Chicken Broth

1 1/2 cups Squash (cubed)

1 (28 oz) can Petite Diced Tomatoes (undrained)

1 (15 oz) can Pinto Beans

1 (15 oz) can Cannellini Beans

1 (15 oz) can Red Kidney Beans (rinsed and drained)

Directions

Broil peppers. While they are cooking:

Heat oil in stockpot, add onion, and cook for 15 minutes, stirring occasionally.

Stir in all spices and garlic, cooking for 2 more minutes.

Add peppers, broth, squash and tomatoes, bring to simmer and cook 20 minutes.

Add beans cook another 20 minutes or so, until squash is desired consistency.

Submitted by: Aimee D

White Bean & Spinach Soup

Servings: 2
Proteins/Carbs/Fats: 1 / 3 / 0

Ingredients

1/2 lb Dried Navy Beans (picked over and rinsed)

2 Tbsp Olive Oil

2 stalks Celery (diced)

3 Carrots (peeled and sliced)

1 Medium Onion (diced)

1 clove Garlic (finely chopped)

2 large strips Turkey Bacon (diced)

46 oz Chicken Broth

1/2 tsp Pepper

1/2 package (5 oz) Chopped Spinach or Kale

Directions

Place beans in large pot and cover beans with water by 2 inches. Bring to boil over high heat; boil 5 minutes. Cover and remove from heat, let stand for 1 hour. Drain remaining water.

Heat oil in large pot or Dutch oven over medium high heat. Add diced turkey bacon and sauté for one minute; add carrots, celery, onion, garlic-stir frequently for 5 minutes. Add drained beans, chicken broth and pepper. Bring to a boil over high heat. Lower heat and simmer for 1 hour.

Remove about 1 cup of beans from soup and mash in a bowl. Return mashed beans to soup.

Add spinach or kale. Bring to boil (high heat) then lower heat and simmer for 10 minutes.

Tip: You can soak the beans overnight, drain and rinse and start at #2.

Submitted by: Paula Siegel

Esther's Vegetable/Bean Soup

Servings: 15
Proteins/Carbs/Fats: 0 / 1 / 0

Ingredients

4 Carrots

4 stalks Celery

1 Large Onion

3 buds Garlic

1 Large Russett Potato (or any kind)

Variety Green Split Peas, Yellow Peas, Lentils, Navy Beans, Lima Beans and Barley

1 box Chicken Soup, Beef Broth, or Vegetable Broth

1 large can Cut-up Stewed Tomatoes

2 tsp Unrefined Sea Salt

1/2 tsp White Pepper

1 1/2 tsp Cumin

1 tsp Dill (fresh or not)

2 tsp Parsley (fresh or not)

1/4 tsp Cayenne Pepper (optional)

Directions

Fill a big soup pot with 12 cups of water; bring to a boil.

Cut up celery, onion, garlic and potato. Add to pot.

In a glass measuring cup, put a variety of green split peas, yellow peas, lentils, navy beans, lima beans and barley. Mix them all together, and add to the water.

Add a box of chicken soup, beef broth, or vegetable broth.

Add a large can of cut-up stewed tomatoes.

All ingredients (except spices) should now be in the pot of water. Cook at low heat for about two hours.

Season to taste. Suggested seasonings include sea salt, white pepper, cumin, dill, parsley and cayenne pepper.

This soup is delicious! It is great to keep in the freezer and reheat as needed.

Submitted by: Esther Feldberg

Pea Soups

Pea & Basil Soup

Servings: 6
Proteins/Carbs/Fats: 0 / 1 / 1

Ingredients

2 Tbsp Olive Oil

1 Tbsp Butter (optional)

1 Small Onion (diced)

1 clove Garlic (minced)

1 tsp Freshly Ground Black Pepper

1 1/2 lbs (about 4 1/2 cups or 2 boxes/bags) Frozen Sweet Peas

3/4 cup Fresh Basil Leaves (chopped)

2 cups Low Sodium Chicken Broth (divided)

1 cup Organic Milk (optional)

4-6 very thin slices Fresh Mozzarella Cheese or Goat Cheese

1/4 cup Roasted Red, Yellow, and Orange Bell Peppers (diced)

To taste Unrefined Sea Salt

Directions

1. Place a medium soup pot over medium heat. Add olive oil, onions, garlic, salt and pepper.

2. Cook until the onions are soft and translucent, about 5 minutes. Add peas and basil, and heat until the peas are thawed.

3. Place pea mixture in a blender. Add 1 cup of the chicken broth and pulse until pureed, adding more broth, if necessary, to puree. Return the pureed mixture to the pot. Stir in the remaining chicken broth. Return the pan to medium heat and cook until hot, but not boiling.

4. To serve, place soup in bowls. Float a thin slice of fresh mozzarella cheese or a little bit of the goat cheese on top of each soup and sprinkle with the diced roasted peppers. Serve immediately.

Sudmitted by: Simone Carrara

Rena's Split Pea Soup

Servings: 4
Proteins/Carbs/Fats: 0 / 1 / 0

Ingredients

1 cup Dried Green Peas

1/4 cup Barley

1/2 cup Carrots (chopped)

1/2 cup Celery (chopped)

1/4 Onion (chopped)

1 (49.5 oz) can + 1 (14 oz) can Chicken Broth

1/2 tsp Herbs from Provence with Lavender (or try Summer Savory) OR 1 tsp dried dill

1/2 tsp Black Pepper

1 tsp Olive Oil

Directions

Saute chopped veggies in olive oil in saucepan.

Remove from pan and set aside.

Add broth, peas and barley to saucepan.

Simmer 45 minutes.

During last 20 minutes, add veggies.

Salt to taste.

* If you desire a thicker pea soup, simmer an additional ½ cup peas with 1 ½ cups water in a separate saucepan for an hour. Mash mixture and add to original pot when done.

Submitted by: Rena Marks

Mrs. Linett's Pea Soup

Servings: 8
Proteins/Carbs/Fats: 0 / 1 / 0

Ingredients

1 cup Green Split Peas (rinsed)

6 cups Water

1 Onion

3 Carrots

3 stalks Celery

To taste Unrefined Sea Salt and Pepper

Tomato Sauce (homemade is best)

Directions

Put the water and vegetables in the pot and cook until the peas are tender (about an hour).

Mush all the vegetables in the pot (use a potato masher).

Add the tomato sauce to taste.

Cook for another 10-15 minutes.

Submitted by: Nan Corbin

Celeriac & Split Pea Soup

Servings: 8
Proteins/Carbs/Fats: 0 / 1 / 0

Ingredients

1 Whole Celeriac Root (roughly diced)

2 Leeks (white part only, thinly sliced)

2 fist-sized Potatoes

1 cup Split Yellow Peas (rinsed and drained)

Butter

32 oz Vegetable Stock*

To taste Black Pepper

To garnish Fresh Chives

*Add more stock for a thinner soup

Directions

Melt a generous table spoon of butter in a large pot over a low heat and gently soften the leeks for 3-4 minutes. Add the celeriac, cover with a sheet of damp greaseproof paper and lid and cook (still on low heat) for 10 minutes.

Remove the lid and paper. Add the potato, split peas and stock to the pan. Cover with the lid, bring to the boil, then reduce heat and simmer for 30 minutes - until the peas are completely cooked.

Whizz the soup in a food processor in batches until it is all smooth (or use a stick blender).

Check the seasoning - the celeriac should have a salty enough taste, so only pepper is needed. Reheat the soup and ladle into bowls; garnish with chives.

Submitted by: Isabel Urch - Glenrothes, Fife, Scotland

Vegetarian Split Pea Soup

Servings: 4
Proteins/Carbs/Fats: 0 / 1 / 0

Ingredients

1 Tbsp Oil (for cooking)

2 Large Onions (chopped)

1/2 tsp Unrefined Sea Salt

2 cups Dried Split Green Peas (picked over and rinsed)

5 cups Water

1/2 Lemon (juiced, reserve the zest)

A few pinches Smoked Paprika

To drizzle Olive Oil

Directions

Add oil to a big pot over medium high heat. Stir in onions and salt; cook until the onions soften, just a minute or two.

Add the split peas and water. Bring to a boil, dial down the heat, and simmer for 20 minutes, or until the peas are cooked through (but still a touch al dente).

Using a large cup or mug, ladle half of the soup into a bowl and set aside.

Using a hand blender (or regular blender) puree the soup that is still remaining in the pot. Stir the reserved (still chunky) soup back into the puree - you should have a soup that is nicely textured. If you need to thin the soup out with more water (or stock), do so a bit at a time.

Stir in the lemon juice and taste. If the soup needs more salt, add more a bit at a time until the flavor of the soup really pops.

Ladle into bowls or cups, and serve each drizzled with olive oil and topped with a good pinch of smoked paprika and a touch of lemon zest.

Submitted by: Lindsay Phillips

French Canadian Pea Soup

Servings: 6
Proteins/Carbs/Fats: 0 / 1 / 0

Ingredients

1 package Smoked Pork Hock or Ham or Turkey Leg, etc.

2 cups Carrots (cut)

1 Onion

2 Celery Stalks

2 cups Rinsed Split Peas (yellow or green)

2 or 3 Bay Leaves

1 pinch Unrefined Sea Salt

1 pinch White Pepper

Directions

Simmer pork hocks in 8-10 cups water for 30 minutes.

Finely chop carrots, onion and celery. A chopper works well here.

Remove pork hocks and cut meat into small pieces when cooled.

Add vegetables, bay leaves and some sea salt and white pepper and simmer 40 minutes more.

Add cut up pork hocs and simmer 20 minutes more.

Remove bay leaves.

Serve with a crusty spelt bread.

Submitted by: John Whittingham - Quebec, Canada

Vegetable Soups

Karen's Cream of Broccoli Soup

Servings: 4
Proteins/Carbs/Fats: 1 / 1 / 0

Ingredients

2 stalks Fresh Broccoli

1/2 Medium Onion

1 stalk Celery

1 cup Water

1 cup Water

1/2 cup Slivered Almonds or Washed Raw Cashews

1 Tbsp Chicken Seasoning

1/2 tsp Unrefined Sea Salt

1/8 tsp Dried Dill

1/8 tsp Marjoram

Directions

Combine broccoli, onion, celery and 1 cup of water in a covered kettle. Cook while making the sauce.

DO NOT OVERCOOK - it changes the flavor and color.

Combine nuts, chicken seasoning, salt, dried dill, marjoram and 1 cup of water in blender until smooth as cream.

Add cooked vegetables, being careful not to burn yourself. Blend until smooth. Add another cup of hot water as needed for desired consistency.

Submitted by: Karen Coppe

Cauliflower Celery Soup

Servings: 6
Proteins/Carbs/Fats: 1 / 1 / 0

Ingredients

1 Onion (chopped)

2 Tbsp Olive Oil, Butter or Ghee

1 head Cauliflower

1 bunch Celery

1/2-1 quart Almond Milk

1/2 cup Coconut Milk (optional)

1-2 quarts Vegetable or Chicken Broth

To taste Unrefined Sea Salt and Pepper

Directions

Sautee/steam chopped onion with olive oil in a large covered soup pan until onions are translucent.

Finely chop the cauliflower and celery (or use a professional veggie chopper). Add to pan along with 1/4-1/2 cup of the broth. Cover.

Steam veggies for about 15 minutes, until tender. Add broth, almond milk and coconut milk. Heat almost to a boil, then simmer for another 15-20 minutes. Add ample amounts of salt and pepper to enhance flavor.

Taking portions at a time, ladle into blender and puree. Be sure not to overfill the blender to avoid hot soup splattering out. Pour each portion into another large container, continuing until all soup is blended. Put in bowls. Serve.

Submitted by: Susie Best - Denver, Colorado

Mom's Ginger Carrot Soup

Servings: 6
Proteins/Carbs/Fats: 0 / 1 / 0

Ingredients

1 large bag Baby Carrots

6 cups Chicken Stock

4 cups Water

1 Medium Onion (diced)

2 cloves Garlic (minced)

1 can Coconut Milk

1 inch Fresh Ginger Root (minced)

1-2 tsp Unrefined Sea Salt (to taste)

To taste Black Pepper

1 tsp Dried Cilantro, or about 1/4 of a bunch fresh (stems removed, minced)

Directions

In a large pot, boil the baby carrots until soft and then discard the water as it is bitter.

Return the soft carrots to the pot and add all ingredients except for the cilantro.

Bring to a boil, then reduce heat and simmer for 45 minutes to an hour.

Puree the soup either with a hand blender, or in the blender/food processor in SMALL BATCHES (large batches will cause the mixture to "explode" from the trapped heat).

Add the cilantro to the soup puree, then taste.

Add additional salt/pepper if desired.

Submitted by: Malissa Rush - Dallas, Texas

Creamless Creamed Roasted Cauliflower Soup

Servings: 6
Proteins/Carbs/Fats: 0 / 1 / 0

Ingredients

1 Cauliflower*

3 cloves Garlic

1 Onion

4-5 Celery Stalks

For cooking Olive Oil, Butter or Ghee

1 cup (or more) Veggie Broth

To taste Unrefined Sea Salt

Bay Leaf

Parsley

Fresh Thyme

*Can substitute with broccoli

Directions

Cut up cauliflower, and roast with garlic and sliced onion for 30 minutes at 400º F.

While roasting, cup to celery. Sautee. Add cauliflower mixture.

Add at least 1 cup of veggie broth and 2 cups of water, along with a little sea salt, bay leaf, parsley and fresh thyme. Simmer for at least 20 minutes.

Take out bay leaf and pour mixture into blender leaving some cauliflower in pieces for texture. Yummy!

Submitted by: Sharon Dietrich - Melbourne, Florida

Stuffed Green Pepper Soup

Servings: 8
Proteins/Carbs/Fats: 2 / 1 / 0

Ingredients

1 lb Ground Beef

1 1/2 cups Onion (diced)

1/2 tsp Basil

1/2 tsp Oregano

1 (14.5 oz) can Diced Tomatoes

1 cup Green Peppers (chopped)

1 (8 oz) can Tomato Paste

3 1/2 cups Water

1 Tbsp Beef Bouillon

1 cup Cooked Brown Rice

To Taste Unrefined Sea Salt and Pepper

Directions

Brown beef with onion; drain any grease. Place in slow cooker with the remaining ingredients.

Cook on low for 6 – 8 hours, or place in large soup pot and simmer for one hour.

Submitted by: Cindy Dickerson - Mansfield, Ohio

Hearty Tomato Soup

Servings: 16
Proteins/Carbs/Fats: 0 / 1 / 0

Ingredients

Olive Oil

1 clove Garlic (minced)

1 Onion (chopped)

1 stalk Celery (chopped)

1 Carrot (chopped)

2 Tbsp Rice Flour

3 cups Tomatoes (chopped) or 1 (28 oz) can Tomatoes (chopped)

To taste Unrefined Sea Salt and Pepper

1 tsp Oregano

1 tsp Basil

1 1/2 cups Cooked Brown Rice

3 cups Hot Milk

1 Tbsp Butter

Directions

In heavy pot, saute garlic, onion, celery and carrot in olive oil. When onion is golden, add rice flour. Stir and saute until toasty.

Add tomatoes, salt and pepper, oregano and basil, and brown rice. Cook at least 15 minutes.

Puree in blender. Add milk, butter, and salt and pepper, as needed. Warm but DO NOT boil.

Serve immediately.

*Can leave out milk and butter.

Submitted by: Jemi - Kyoto, Japan

Honeymoon Vegetable Soup

Servings: 8
Proteins/Carbs/Fats: 2 / 1 / 0

Ingredients

1 lb Stewing Beef (cubed in small pieces)

1 (28 oz) can Whole or Crushed Tomatoes

4 Carrots (chopped)

1/2 cup Onion (diced)

4 stalks Celery (chopped)

1 Tbsp Whole Allspice ("balls")

To taste Unrefined Sea Salt and Pepper

Directions

Rinse and boil the beef in the water (to make the broth) until almost done, in large saucepan.

Add the carrots, celery, onion and tomatoes. Add whole allspice, salt and pepper. Bring to a boil and simmer 30 minutes or until vegetables are soft.

Take a tablespoon and remove all whole allspice balls. The secret to the flavor is in using whole allspice!

Submitted by: Sheralee Iglehart - California

Roasted Red Pepper Soup

Servings: 6
Proteins/Carbs/Fats: 0 / 1 / 0

Ingredients

3 Large Red Peppers (cut up)

2 Plum Tomatoes (halved lengthwise)

1 Onion (quartered)

3 Large Garlic Cloves (peeled)

1 Tbsp Olive Oil

1 (15 oz) can Chicken Broth

1 tsp Balsamic Vinegar

1/4 tsp Unrefined Sea Salt

1/8 tsp Freshly Ground Pepper

1/4 cup Basil (very thinly sliced for garnish)

Directions

Preheat oven to 425° F.

Toss peppers, tomatoes, onions, and garlic with the oil.

Spread on a broiler pan in a single layer, and roast for 30 minutes until vegetables are tender and carmelized.

Let cool and peel skin off of tomatoes and peppers.

Transfer vegetables to a sauce pan and add broth, bring to a simmer.

Cover and cook for 10 minutes.

Transfer to a blender or use an emersion blender right in the pan.

Add vinegar, salt and pepper.

Puree the vegetables for about a minute or until it is a thick sauce type texture. If using a blender then return soup to the pan and cook just until it is heated through.

Garnish with a small nest of basil in the center of the bowl.

DELISH!!!!

Submitted by: Becky Heidel - Somers, Montana

Minestrone Italiano

Servings: 10
Proteins/Carbs/Fats: 0 / 1 / 0

Ingredients

3 Tbsp Olive Oil, Butter or Ghee (for cooking)

1 Medium Onion (chopped)

1 cup Potatoes (diced)

1 cup Celery (sliced)

1 cup Carrots (sliced)

1 (15 oz) can Diced Tomatoes

1 (15 oz) can White Beans (drained)

2 Bay Leaves

2 Vegetable or Chicken Broth Boullion Cubes

To taste Unrefined Sea Salt & Pepper

*Cabbage or cauliflower may also be added

Directions

Heat oil. Add onion, potatoes, celery, carrots and tomatoes. Sauté for 2 minutes. Cover with hot water.

Add 2 boullion cubes; simmer, covered, until tender (about 1-2 hours).

Add beans, bay leaves, salt and pepper. Cook on low for another 15 minutes.

Submitted by: Liz Ambrose - Great Falls, Montana

Carrot & Orange Soup

Servings: 8
Proteins/Carbs/Fats: 0 / 1 / 0

Ingredients

2 Tbsp Butter

2 cups Yellow Onions (finely chopped)

12 Large Carrots (peeled and chopped)

6 cups Chicken Stock (divided)

1 cup Freshly Squeezed Orange Juice

To taste Unrefined Sea Salt and Pepper

To taste Orange Zest

Directions

Melt the butter in a pot. Add the onions, cover and cook over low heat until tender and lightly cooked – about 25 minutes.

Add carrots and four cups of stock, and bring to the boil. Reduce heat. Cover and simmer until carrots are very tender – about 30 minutes.

Remove from heat and process with a stick blender or Vita Mix until very smooth. Add orange juice and additional chicken stock until soup is of desired consistency.

Season to taste with salt and pepper. Add orange zest, and simmer until heated through.

Submitted by: Jean McCullough - Alberta, Canada

Tomato Basil Soup

Servings: 8
Proteins/Carbs/Fats: 0 / 1 / 0

Ingredients

2 (28 oz) cans Tomatoes

2 cloves Garlic (roughly chopped)

1/2 cup Fresh Basil (roughly chopped)

2 cups Low-Sodium, Free-Range Chicken Broth

To taste Unrefined Sea Salt and Pepper

To taste Raw Honey or Stevia

Directions

Put all ingredients in a food processor (except salt, pepper & honey) and pulse 3-4 times or until creamy.

Transfer to a pan, and simmer on low heat for 15 minutes, or until warm. Season to taste.

Submitted by: Rhonda - Kansas City, Missouri

Meat & Vegetable Soups

Stacie & Jeff's Turkey Vegetable Soup

Servings: 6
Proteins/Carbs/Fats: 3 / 2 / 0

Ingredients

2 cloves Garlic (minced)

2 Large Carrots (chopped)

3 Medium Potatoes (chopped)

1 Medium Onion (chopped)

1 Green Bell Pepper (chopped)

1 Red Bell Pepper (chopped)

1 Orange Bell Pepper (chopped)

1 Medium Head of Cabbage (chopped)

2 cups Chicken Broth

4 cups Water

1 lb Ground Turkey

Directions

Brown ground turkey in skillet.

Over medium high heat, add garlic, carrots, potatoes, onion and bell peppers to stockpot. Cook until vegetables are tender, approximately 15 minutes, stirring occasionally.

Add cabbage, chicken broth, water and turkey. Heat to boiling over high heat, stirring occasionally.

Reduce heat to low. Cover and simmer, approximately 15 minutes, or until all vegetables are tender.

Submitted by: Stacie & Jeff Matthews - Midland, TX

Easy Slow Cooker Hamburger Soup

Servings: 12
Proteins/Carbs/Fats: 3 / 1 / 0

Ingredients

2 lbs Ground Beef or Bison

4 tsp Garlic (minced)

1 cup Onions (diced)

1 cup Celery (diced)

3 (19 oz) cans Organic Diced Tomatoes

2 cups Organic Frozen Vegetables of Choice

2 tsp Basil

2 tsp Cilantro

1 cup Mushrooms (sliced)

Directions

Brown ground beef/bison with the minced garlic, onions and mushrooms. Add to slow cooker. Add remaining ingredients to slow cooker. Cook on high for 1 hour. Lower heat to low and cook a minimum of 3 hours.

To add a little kick, or for a change of pace, taco seasoning can be added to the ground beef/bison as it is being browned.

Submitted by: Tracy - Winnipeg, Manitoba, Canada

Carolyn's Fish Soup

Servings: 8
Proteins/Carbs/Fats: 1 / 1 / 0

Ingredients

1 Tbsp Olive Oil

1 tsp Butter

1 cup Peppers (red and yellow, chopped)

1/2 cup Celery (chopped)

1 Tbsp Parsley (dry)

To taste Unrefined Sea Salt and Pepper

1 Bay Leaf

2 Medium Potatoes (peeled and grated, adds thickness but optional)

3 cups Chicken or Vegetable Broth

1 cup Cold Water

2 cups White Fish (Cod, Haddock, Tilapia, chopped), Wild Salmon, Shrimp, Scallops (either fresh or frozen)

Directions

Saute onion, peppers, and celery in heated oil and melted butter over medium heat until soft but not brown.

Add seasonings (including bay leaf) and liquid. Bring to a boil. Add grated potato (if using) and simmer 30 minutes.

Add fish and cook 5 minutes longer. Remove bay leaf before serving. This dish is tasty if left and reheated next day.

Submitted by: Carolyn Marshall - St. John's, Newfoundland, Canada

Judy's Hearty Ham & Beet Soup

Servings: 8
Proteins/Carbs/Fats: 1 / 1 / 0

Ingredients

1 1/2 cups Beets (chopped)

4 stalks Celery (chopped)

1/4 cup Lean Ground Pork

1 cup Ham (any cut, chopped)

2 large or 3 medium Carrots (chopped)

1 Medium Onion or 1/2 Large Onion (chopped)

1 cup Broccoli Florets (washed)

For ground pork seasoning
Unrefined Sea Salt and Pepper

2 cups Water

2 cups Hot Water (to add later)

1 tsp Dried Parsley

2 tsp 5-Spice Powder

1 tsp Cinnamon

1/2 tsps Sesame Oil

1 tsp Butter

*Can substitue turkey, chicken, veal, buffalo, or beef for pork

Directions

In a small bowl add the lean ground pork, a pinch of salt and pepper and lightly mix with a spoon; set aside.

Bring 2 cups of water to a boil; add the beets. Cook for about 5-10 minutess, until the color starts to come out of the beets (water becomes bright red). Then turn the heat down to about medium low. Add the carrots, celery and the other 2 cups of hot water; let simmer for about 5 minutes. In a small pan add the butter and onions; saute the onions on medium low until slightly caramelized. Add onions, ham, and pork mixture to the pot of soup one scoop at a time. Add in the dried parsley, 5-spice powder, cinnamon and sesame oil. Let it all come to a boil and then turn the heat to medium low; let it simmer for about 1 1/2 to 2 hours. Make sure you put a lid on the pot while it's simmering but leave an opening for air. In the same pan used to cook the onions, add the broccoli florets without any liquid or oil. Cover it with a lid to steam (on medium high) for about 5-10 minutes, until tender; set aside until the soup is fully cooked and every ingredient is tender and full of flavor. Once the soup is done, add salt and pepper to taste and ladle each serving into a bowl and garnish with 1 or 2 pieces of broccoli in the middle.

Submitted by: Judy Tiet

"The Best" Italian Turkey Vegetable Soup

Servings: 8
Proteins/Carbs/Fats: 2 / 3 / 0

Ingredients

2 Tbsp Olive Oil, Butter or Ghee (for cooking)

1 Large Onion (chopped)

4 Celery Stalks (diced into 1/4 inch pieces)

2 cloves Garlic (pressed)

1 quart Chicken Broth (or vegetable broth)

2 (28 oz) cans Diced Tomatoes (or use one can of tomato sauce)

2 (15 oz) cans Kidney Beans (drained and rinsed)

1 lb White Mushrooms (sliced)

1 can Ripe Olives (sliced)

4 cups Dark Turkey Meat (chopped)

3-4 Bay Leaves

3 Tbsp Dried Oregano (or to taste)

3 Small Zucchini (sliced)

6 oz Spinach (washed)

Directions

Saute onion and celery in oil in large soup pot.

Add the next eight ingredients. Add additional water and/or broth to desired soupiness. Simmer 30-60 minutes.

Add zucchini and spinach during the last 10 minutes just before serving (these cook very quickly).

Submitted by: Kathy

Thanksgiving Turkey Soup

Servings: 8
Proteins/Carbs/Fats: 2 / 3 / 0

Ingredients

2 Medium Large Onions

8 stalks Celery

1 Medium Rutabaga

6 Parsnips

10 Carrots

4 cups Water

4 boxes Stock

Leftover Turkey Carcass

Red Pepper Flakes

Dried Dill Weed

Fresh Parsley

Directions

After removing most of the breast meat for Thanksgiving dinner, simmer the carcass with the wings and legs in 4 cups of water and 4 boxes of stock.

Chop the onions, celery, rutabaga, parsnips and carrots. Add to pot.

Remove the bones, and chop the turkey. Added the chopped turkey back into the soup after 2-3 hours of cooking. Season the soup with red pepper flakes and dried dill weed to taste. Garnish with fresh parsley.

Submitted by: Dianne Lambart - Michigan

Nonna's All Day Minestrone

Servings: 10
Proteins/Carbs/Fats: 4 / 2 / 0

Ingredients

2-3 lb Chuck Steak

1 Tbsp Olive Oil

2 Tbsp Butter

1 Medium Yellow Onion (diced)

4-5 cloves Garlic (minced)

6 cups Water

2 (32 oz) cartons Beef Broth

1 (32 oz) carton Vegetable Broth

1 tsp Dried Basil

1/2 tsp Dried Oregano

1/4 tsp each Dried Thyme, Dried Marjoram, Fresh Rosemary (chopped)

1 tsp Pepper

1 small can Tomato Paste

1 (14.5 oz) can Diced Tomatoes

3 stalks Celery (diced)

3 Thin Carrots (diced chunkey)

3-4 Roma Tomatoes (diced)

2 Zucchini (diced chunky)

8-10 Button Mushrooms (stemmed and quartered)

1 (15 oz) can Garbanzo Beans (rinsed and drained)

1 (15 oz) can Cannellini or Kidney Beans (rinsed and drained)

3/4 cup Frozen Petite Peas (thawed)

1 1/2 cup Fresh Green Beans (cut to bite size pieces)

2-3 handfuls Spinach

2 cups Shredded Savoy Cabbage

1 1/2-1 3/4 cup Isabel Approved Pasta, (elbow or shells, optional)

Directions

Trim meat of excess fat and cut into hand size chunks; salt and pepper, to taste. In a large stock pot (10-12 quarts) add oil and butter over medium heat. Brown chunks of meat removing and setting aside until all meat is browned. Add onions and garlic to the pot and sweat until softened. Add meat back to the pot. Add water, 1 carton each of beef and vegetable broths, tomato paste, diced tomatoes, basil, oregano, thyme, marjoram and rosemary. Simmer on low for approximately 3 hours.

Prep other vegetables. Place in bowls, ready to add.

After 3 hours, pull meat from soup and set aside. Add carrots and celery. Chunk meat apart (bite sized) and add back to soup. Add ½ of a carton of beef broth, Roma tomatoes, mushrooms and zucchini; simmer 20 minutes. Add canned beans, green beans and peas; simmer 15 minutes. Add cabbage and spinach; simmer 30 minutes. Add pasta; simmer another 15-30 minutes, making sure all the vegetables are cooked down enough.

This makes a large batch of soup which can last all week or you can freeze some for later.

Submitted by: Tina Walker McCullom - Roseville, CA

Beef & Barley Soup

Servings: 6
Proteins/Carbs/Fats: 5 / 1 / 0

Ingredients

2 lbs Ground Turkey

1 (16 oz) can Tomatoes (chopped)

7 cups Water

1/2 lb Green Beans (halved)

1 Green Pepper (sliced)

1/2 cup Celery (sliced)

1/2 cup Celery Greens

2 Carrots (sliced)

2 tsp Garlic Powder

1 Bay Leaf

1/2 tsp Paprika

1/2 tsp Thyme

2 Chicken Bouillon Cubes

1/2 cup Pearl Barley

To taste Unrefined Sea Salt and Pepper

Directions

Brown meat in large soup pot.

Add everything else.

Simmer until carrots are tender.

Submitted by: Jody Andrews - Melbourne, Florida

Randy's Hearty Hamburger Soup

Servings: 12
Proteins/Carbs/Fats: 2 / 1 / 0

Ingredients

1 1/2 lb Ground Beef

1-2 Onions (chopped)

2 cloves Garlic (minced)

2 cans Diced Tomatoes

4 cups Beef Broth

2 cups Water

6 Carrots (chopped in coins)

4 ribs Celery (chopped)

1 tsp Thyme

1 tsp Oregano

2 Bay Leaves

1/2 tsp Fire Roasted Tomatoes

1/2 tsp Chipotle Pepper Flakes

8 Tbsp Barley (use brown rice for a gluten-free soup)

Directions

Brown meat, onions and garlic. Drain if necessary.

Combine all ingredients in large Dutch oven and simmer, covered, stirring occasionally at least 2-3 hours.

Can be frozen and reheated at a later time.

Submitted by: Randy Styles - Barrie, Ontario, Canada

Moroccan Vegetable Soup (Chorba)

Servings: 8
Proteins/Carbs/Fats: 2 / 1 / 0

Ingredients

2 Tbsp Olive Oil, Butter or Ghee

1 Medium Onion (finely diced)

2 tsp Ground Tumeric

1 lb Beef Stew Meat or Lamb Stew Meat (trimmed and cut into 1/2 inch pieces)

6 cups Beef Broth or Water

1 (14 oz) can Diced Tomatoes

2 Small Turnips (peeled and diced)

2 Carrots (diced)

2 stalks Celery (leaves included, thinly sliced)

1 pinch Saffron Threads

12 sprigs Flat-Leaf Parsley (plus more leaves for garnish)

8 sprigs Fresh Cilantro (plus more leaves for garnish)

1 Large Zucchini (peeled and cut into 1/4 inch dice)

1-2 tsp Unrefined Sea Salt (or to taste)

1/2 tsp Freshly Ground Pepper

Directions

Heat oil in a Dutch oven over medium-high heat. Add onion and tumeric; stir to coat. Add meat and cook, stirring occasionally, until the onion is tender, 4-5 minutes. Add broth (or water), tomatoes and their juice, turnips, carrots, celery and saffron. Tie parsley and cilantro sprigs together with kitchen string and add to the pot. Bring the soup to a boil. Cover and reduce to a simmer. Cook until the meat is tender, 45-50 minutes.

Stir in zucchini and cook, covered, until soft, 8-10 minutes. Discard the parsley and cilantro sprigs. Season with salt (start with 1 teaspoon if using beef broth; add more if using water) and pepper. Serve sprinkled with parsley and/or cilantro leaves, if desired.

Variations: Feel free to add or substitute whatever vegetables you have handy or like. Some ideas: kale, leeks, kohlrabi, bell peppers, peas, green beans. Make mini-meatballs to sbustitute for other cuts of meat.

Submitted by: Mary

Beef & Cabbage Soup (with an Indian touch)

Servings: 8
Proteins/Carbs/Fats: 2 / 1 / 0

Ingredients

1 lb Beef (cut into cubes)

2 cups Cabbage (chopped)

1 cup Celery (chopped)

2 Large Tomatoes (chopped)

1 Large Sweet Potato (peeled and sliced)

3-4 cups Chicken Stock

For cooking Olive Oil

1 Large Red Onion (chopped)

3-4 cloves Garlic (minced)

1 inch piece Fresh Ginger (grated)

1 tsp Chili Powder

1 tsp Cumin Powder

2 tsp Coriander Powder

1 tsp Turmeric Powder

1 tsp Cinnamon Powder

Directions

Combine the first 6 ingredients (beef, cabbage, celery, tomatoes, sweet potato, and chicken stock) in a slow cooker. Start cooking at high heat.

Meanwhile, heat 2 tablespoons olive oil in a skillet and saute the onions, garlic and ginger until the onions are soft. Put onions, garlic and ginger into the pot along with the spices. Cook until the meat is soft, about 3 hours.

Add the coconut milk towards the end of the cooking. Season with freshly ground black pepper and sea salt.

Note: Can cook in regular stock pot or even in a large pressure cooker, whichever is convenient for you.

Submitted by: Molly Mammen

Salmon, Baby Corn & Mushroom Soup

Servings: 3
Proteins/Carbs/Fats: 3 / 1 / 0

Ingredients

1 Large Wild Salmon Fish Head or 9 oz Salmon Fish with Lots of Bones

8-10 pices (or 6 oz) Non-GMO Baby Corn

4 oz Shiitake Mushrooms and Willow Mushrooms (or any strong tasting mushrooms)

To taste Unrefined Sea Salt

Directions

Wash ingredients.

Boil salmon fish in alkaline water/filtered water (3/4 full of a medium pot). Remove the particles that float up to the surface and simmer for 30 minutes.

Put in organic baby corn and simmer for another 30 minutes. (The baby corn minimizes the pungent smell of the salmon.)

Put in mushrooms and simmer for another 60 minutes or more. Add salt to taste.

Tips: Stir the soup every 20-30 minutes to make sure the richness of the ingredients are diffused thoroughly. The longer the soup simmers, the tastier the soup. I took 3 hours to get the taste I desired.

Submitted by: Frieda Loh

Mom's Noodle Soup

Servings: 8
Proteins/Carbs/Fats: 4 / 1 / 0

Ingredients

Noodles:

5 Egg Yolks

Sprouted Grain Flour

Beef Soup:

1 1/2 - 2 lbs Braised Beef

1 large can Whole Tomatoes

2 Tbsp Unrefined Sea Salt

Black Peppercorns

1 Yellow Onion

6 Carrots (peeled)

2 Bay Leaves

Directions

Noodles:

Add sprouted grain flour to egg yolks enough a little at a time to make a stiff dough. Knead the dough on a floured surface until dough is smooth. Divide dough into 5 equal parts and roll each part on a floured surface until very thin. Roll each part into a tube shape. With a sharp knife, slice the rolls into very thin noodles. Toss the sliced noodles together after each roll is sliced to separate the noodles.

In a large pot filled with at least 10 cups of boiling water, place the sliced noodles (approximately one cup at a time). Boil for 1 or 2 minutes. Place noodles in a strainer and run cool water over them to wash clean. Place each batch of washed noodles in a bowl to collect all cooked noodles to await for use in soup.

Beef Soup:

In a large pot (or slow cooker), place braised beef (soup meat with bone preferred). Add one large can of whole tomatoes. Fill empty can twice, and dump into pot. Add salt, to taste. Add several black peppercorns, 1 whole yellow onion, carrots and bay leaves. Bring to boil in a covered pot or slow cooker.

In a slow cooker, turn to high and simmer for 4 hours.

In a covered pot, turn heat to low and simmer for 4 hours.

To serve: Place noodles in serving bowl. Add carrots and pieces of beef. Remove bay leaves from soup, and ladle soup over noodles using a strainer to obtain soup without tomato pieces or peppercorn. Add additional salt to taste.

Submitted by: Joseph Mackovjak

So...just who is Isabel De Los Rios?

Isabel De Los Rios is a certified nutritionist and exercise specialist who has already helped more than 300,000 people all over the world lose incredible

amounts of weight, regain their health and permanently change their lives. She is the author of The Beyond Diet Program and has become the #1 "go-to girl" when it comes to fat-burning nutrition by several of the most popular fitness professionals around the globe. Isabel's cutting-edge and completely different approach to nutrition is what sets her apart from all the rest. Her strategies work, hands down, as long as her simple principles are followed.

Isabel found her passion for nutrition as a teenager. The overweight daughter and granddaughter of type 2 diabetics, Isabel was told she was doomed to suffer from the same health problems as the generations who preceded her. Not willing to sit around waiting for this grim prediction to become a reality, she pored over every nutrition and diet book available in search of the answers to her family's weight and health problems. This led her to personally seek out doctors and health professionals that were using nutrition to get great results (as far as health and weight loss) with their patients and clients.

Isabel is able to educate clients and readers all over the world through her books, hundreds of online articles, seminars, and the media, focusing on the essential principles of fat-loss nutrition and achieving a healthy, toned, and vibrant body.

Isabel graduated from Rutgers University with a degree in exercise physiology (a pre-med curriculum). She is a Certified Strength and Conditioning Specialist, the highest and most advanced certification given by the National Strength and Conditioning Association. She is also a Holistic Nutrition Lifestyle Coach, certified by the Corrective Holistic Exercise

Kinesiology (C.H.E.K.) Institute in San Diego, California. She counsels many special populations, including people with diabetes and heart disease, cancer survivors, and overweight individuals, as well as healthy individuals who wish to maintain their health and prevent disease.

She has since reached and maintained an ideal weight, is vibrantly healthy, and shows no indication that conditions like diabetes will affect her as they have so many in her family. She truly enjoys a high level of well-being that not only surprises most people, but motivates them to achieve what Isabel has.

Notes:

Notes:

Notes:

Notes:

Notes:

Notes:

Notes:

Notes: